DISK
DETECTIVE

DISK
DETECTIVE

```
01101101001011
10101010101010
10101111010110
00010110101000
10100010100100
10100010101011
101000101110
```

Secrets You Must Know to Recover
Information from a Computer

Norbert Zaenglein

PALADIN PRESS • BOULDER, COLORADO

Also by Norbert Zaenglein:

Secret Software

Disk Detective: Secrets You Must Know to Recover Information from a Computer
by Norbert Zaenglein

Copyright © 1998 by Norbert Zaenglein
ISBN 0-87364-992-3
Printed in the United States of America

Published by Paladin Press, a division of
Paladin Enterprises, Inc.
Gunbarrel Tech Center
7077 Winchester Circle
Boulder, Colorado 80301 USA
+1.303.443.7250

Direct inquiries and/or orders to the above address.

PALADIN, PALADIN PRESS, and the "horse head" design
are trademarks belonging to Paladin Enterprises and
registered in United States Patent and Trademark Office.

Visit our Web site at www.paladin-press.com

Table of Contents

Introduction   1

Chapter 1: Exploring the Data Deletion Myth   3

Chapter 2: Introduction to Data Recovery   23

Chapter 3: Recovering from Format   29

Chapter 4: Advanced Search Techniques   39

Chapter 5: Retracing Visited Internet Sites   51

Chapter 6: Password Recovery   71

Chapter 7: More about Passwords   85

Chapter 8: Other Tips and Tricks   93

Conclusion   103

Warning

The examples in this book were performed using specific versions of software on computers running under DOS 6.2, Windows 95 and Windows 3.1. The software, configurations, disk drive assignments, operating systems, and locations of files and folders, and preference settings on other computers may be different from the examples in this book. Therefore, the procedures outlined in this book may not apply to other computers. The reader is cautioned to consult original software manuals for specific instructions and directions for performing any data recovery procedures, including those outlined in this book.

This book is not intended to be a substitute for the expertise of a trained data investigator or forensic data recovery expert. Nor is this book intended to serve as a step-by-step procedural guide for conducting any kind of computer investigation. The actual investigation of any computer must never be done on the original computer or original disk or storage media. Any computer investigation must be performed on an exact duplicate of the disk being investigated.

Do not format, unformat, delete, undelete, wipe, modify, or perform *any* data recovery or investigative procedure outlined in this book unless you do so on a dedicated computer that contains absolutely no useful data or information. Individuals wishing to practice *any* data recovery or investigative exercises, including those outlined in this book, must do so only at a training institution, such as a technical college or university, and then only with the advice, guidance, and consent of a qualified instructor. Always refer to specific software manuals and computer manuals for directions on how to conduct any procedures, including the data recovery and investigative procedures outlined in this book.

Failure to follow specific hardware and software manuals or failure to consult a data recovery expert or forensic data investigation professional prior to performing any data recovery or investigative exercises, including those outlined in this book, may result in overwriting/deleting information, modifying date and time stamps, compromising evidence, or deleting some or all information on a computer.

Furthermore, the improper or illegal investigating of computers might make the evidence gained from such an investigation inadmissible in a court of law.

Always seek the advice of a forensic data recovery expert and legal counsel before performing any computer investigation, data recovery exercises, or investigative techniques. Illegal searches, seizures, data recovery/investigative procedures, or invasion of another person's privacy may subject the person, the investigator, or his agency to litigation or criminal prosecution.

The author and publisher assume no liability in regard to any information contained in this book, including errors and omissions, or for damages resulting from the use of information contained in this book. All know trademarks have been capitalized.

Introduction

The objective of this book is to offer a general overview of computer information recovery for IBM-compatible personal computers. Specifically this publication is designed to help private detectives, parents, teachers, business owners, and law enforcement professionals understand the kind of information that can be recovered. We also examine the basic framework that makes data and information recovery possible by exploring how to recover passwords, restore deleted files, retrace visited Internet sites, recover e-mail messages, and conduct key word searches, as well as how to perform other nonforensic investigative techniques.

Today, there is a growing variety of forensic software on the market. These programs, however, are prohibitively expensive, and their sale is often restricted to law enforcement or individuals who have undergone special training. Restricting the access to forensic software in this manner prevents the large majority of private investigators, parents, teachers, business owners, law enforcement professionals, and interested individuals from studying the subject of information recovery.

To bring the secrets of information recovery into the mainstream, this book includes detailed examples of how information recovery procedures were performed on my computer using software that can be readily purchased by anyone, without any restrictions. Remember, the techniques outlined in this book are for general educational purposes only and *do not* constitute procedures for conducting any computer investigation, especially a forensic computer investigation. An actual forensic investigation must be done by trained individuals using clearly defined procedures, which are not outlined in this book.

The reader should also note that due to the variation in computer setups, user configurations, operating systems, software variations, and user preference settings, the examples in this book may not apply to other computers. For example, on most computers, drive A is a designated floppy disk drive. A computer user, however, can change disk drive assignments and make drive A the hard drive. As a result, an action performed on drive A will instead be performed on the hard disk. The act of formatting drive A would therefore format the hard disk, with subsequent loss of information. Such a scenario may be unlikely, but it is entirely possible. Keep this in mind when studying the examples outlined in this book.

The reader should not assume, and the author does not imply, that the software used to formulate the examples in this book is specifically designed for, or is suitable for, investigative purposes or even for the purposes for which this software is demonstrated in this book. To determine the suitability and appropriate use of *any* software, including the software referenced in this book, the reader must refer to the original software manual or contact the software manufacturer for details.

If you have a favorite information recovery procedure you'd like to share, visit the author's web site at http://www.diskdetectives.com.

Chapter One

Exploring the Data Deletion Myth

Personal computers are an increasingly common commodity in our society. More than one hundred million personal computers are in use today, and their numbers will continue to multiply at a frantic rate well into the next century and beyond. As the numbers of computers increase, so will the importance of understanding computer investigation and data recovery techniques. Private investigators, employers, parents, teachers, and law enforcement professionals must know what kind of information can be recovered, as well as the framework and procedures that make information access and recovery possible.

Computer storage—including hard disks, floppy disks, and backup devices—can harbor valuable evidence or information that can be extracted by a trained professional. Computers and data storage media, like diskettes and backup tapes, can be the repository of evidence, as in the fictitious case discussed later in this book where a killer used his computer to correspond with his victim.

Information recovery is also an important topic for today's business owners and managers. For example, what happens when an employee leaves a firm and does not reveal the password to the company's payroll program? An employer may also have to determine if an employee is transmitting proprietary or copyright information to a competitor.

Today's parents also have legitimate concerns about their children's computer activities. Adult strangers seek out and communicate with minors over the Internet and send inappropriate material or may even lure them away from home. It has happened, and it will happen again.

Teachers and educational institutions also have a vested interest in the activities taking place on computers at their institutions. Suppose a high school student uses the school's computer lab to create false identification papers. He then uses those papers to purchase alcohol and gets into a vehicle accident resulting in a loss of life. Will the school be liable?

Computers can also be an important source for personality profiling for law enforcement and private detectives. An investigator can learn the intimate details about someone by spending a few hours examining that individual's personal computer.

For law enforcement personnel, evidence and information extracted from a computer can jump-start an ongoing criminal investigation, bring a stalled investigation back on track, or provide invaluable insights into illegal activities. A private detective investigating the disappearance of a runaway teenager, for example, may be able to uncover important leads by retracing Internet sites that were visited by the missing teen. Discovering that a runaway has visited the Web site of a bizarre religious cult in California is valuable information that might never be uncovered by any other means. Investigators might also discover valuable evidence by searching for key words in an abduction case where a minor is lured away by an adult with whom the minor had been corresponding over the Internet. Computer-savvy detectives will know how to tap e-mail messages (if the law permits), even those messages protected by passwords. This new breed of detectives will know how to find specific information in slack areas and hidden files using "keyword" searches or bring deleted information back to life. These detectives will know the secrets to cracking a variety of passwords to find out if an employee is embezzling funds. Even though the investigator, employer, or parent may not perform the actual investigation, this book will provide valuable insights into the information recovery process in terms of what can be recovered and the basic framework that makes information recovery possible. Armed with this understanding, the investigator, employer, teacher, or parent will be able to make informed decisions and will better understand the work performed by trained data recovery experts.

Computer investigation and data recovery have enormous implications for private investigators and law enforcement personnel. Computer users entrust their most private information to their computers, including personal letters and love notes, business and financial records, even unlawful sexual material. What few computer users understand is that once information is accessed by a computer, or once such information is stored on a computer, there is a good chance that portions of this information can be recovered, even after it has been deleted. Yet only a handful of investigators are taking heed of these new investigative opportunities. Few, if any, law enforcement training programs cover the topic of computer seizures or, at the very least, teach officers about the evidence computers might yield. Despite the proliferation in computers, many law enforcement officers and private investigators minimize the importance of the computer as an investigative tool.

Without a solid foundation in computer investigation, private detectives and police departments will fall far behind the technology curve, missing out on important leads and valuable evidence. The old "gum-shoe" techniques will always play a role in solving crimes, but the future will see a breed of detectives who understand computers and their role in a variety of investigations. These new detectives will know that deleted evidence can be recovered and that valuable leads to finding a missing child may be just a few clicks of the mouse away.

The key that makes information recovery possible is that the vast majority of computer users do not realize that the information they deleted last week, or even last year, can still be recovered. Sometimes even information that the computer user never saved to a disk can be recovered! That may surprise even some experienced computer users, but it's true. Take this chapter that I am writing. This chapter is written using Microsoft Word. What would happen if I stopped writing this book right now without ever saving this file? Even if I had never saved this chapter to a file, the information could still be recovered!

Many computer users do not understand just how difficult it is to fully delete information or to protect information from prying eyes. Most individuals assume that if they delete a file, overwrite a file, or format a disk containing a file, the information will be deleted. That assumption obviously must be wrong, or there would be no material for this book. It can, in fact, be pretty difficult for the average user to delete all remnants of information once stored on a computer.

One thing to remember is that the laws pertaining to computer searches and seizures are complex, sometimes contradictory, and constantly evolving. Computer searches and seizures must be conducted lawfully and in accordance with the regulations of each jurisdiction. Each investigator must be familiar with local laws governing computer investigation before seizing, storing, or investigating computers. Some electronic information, such as electronic communications, may be governed by special statutory rules and is off limits.

We begin our journey into the intriguing world of computer investigation by examining how to recover deleted information. To make the data recovery exercises in this book more interesting, we will be using a fictitious murder case. In this imaginary homicide, the computer is the repository of the evidence that is needed to get a first-degree murder conviction. This book will follow a fictional suspect as he tries to delete incriminating letters that link him to the victim. We follow investigators and watch as they recover the evidence that the suspect tries to destroy by using several means.

Many of the data recovery exercises in this book will be performed on IBM-compatible computers running Windows 95, Windows 3.1, DOS 6.2, and Netscape 2 and 3. There are several compelling reasons to include procedures for Windows 3.1 and DOS. First, DOS and Windows 3.x continue to be used in a large number of computers today. Second, understanding data recovery processes for such operating systems as Windows 3.1 and DOS lays the foundation for advanced data recovery methods outlined in subsequent chapters. Third, the Windows 95 Recycle Bin may make it simple to initially recover deleted files. But what about files deleted from floppies or those emptied from the Recycle Bin? To restore such information requires procedures similar to those required to restore files deleted in DOS and Windows 3.x. Furthermore, you cannot always rely on the Windows 95 Recycle Bin to protect all deleted files. Certain files, like those deleted through DOS or individual software programs, can quite easily escape Recycle Bin protection.

As we venture into the intriguing world of data recovery, pretend that you are a new detective in a precinct where a murder investigation is under way. It's 7:45 A.M. on your first day of duty. The chief calls you into his office. Holding a steaming cup of coffee, you sit down at the cluttered table. The chief introduces you to your partner, Mike M., a seasoned homicide investigator. Mike briefs you on the case by taking you back to January 3, 1998.

January 3, 1998, 4:02 P.M.: Sally G., a 26-year-old school

Disk Detective

teacher who lives alone in a small apartment, is distraught because she received a disturbing letter. The unidentified writer said that he had seen Sally and fallen in love with her. The writer wants to meet Sally sometime in the future, but for now the writer warns Sally that there will be grave consequences if she dates anyone else. Detective Mike M. questions Sally about who she thought may have written the letter. Sally doesn't have a clue. Then, just before leaving the office, she mentions an incident that took place at a bar about three months earlier. Sally went out for a birthday drink with a friend. At the bar, a small man with bushy red hair and an unkempt appearance approached Sally on several occasions, asking her to dance and to go out with him. Sally politely declined, but the man kept pursuing her. As the man became more intoxicated, he became aggressive and belligerent. He grabbed Sally's arm and tried to force her to dance. There was a scuffle, and the bartender and two other men stepped in. When Sally and her friend left the bar, they were escorted by the bartender, who told Sally that he had no idea who the man was. She recalled the bartender looking around at the cars parked in front of the bar and that there was a large, blue, four-wheel drive truck with out-of-area plates. After Sally and her friend drove off, the bartender threw the man out of his bar and told him never to come back.

February 12, 1998, 11:38 A.M.: Detective Mike M. is finishing a report on a vehicle theft when the phone rings. It's Sally. She has received another letter, a long rambling note full of sexual innuendoes and loving language. The letter demands that Sally drive to a nearby shopping mall on February 14 so the two of them can meet and talk things out. The writer states that there will be serious consequences if she does not show up at the appointed time. Sally has no intention of going to the meeting.

8

Exploring the Data Deletion Myth

March 21, 1998, 11:38 A.M.: Sally receives another letter. The writer found out that Sally is dating someone. The writer warns Sally to stop dating immediately and that if she does not, he will kill her.

The writer left no fingerprints on any of the letters, and he used self-sticking postage stamps and self-sealing envelopes to avoid DNA recovery. The investigation has also determined that the letters were not written on a manual typewriter but were, instead, printed on a laser printer.

April 7, 1998, 11:38 A.M.: Sally marries John Smith in a small, quiet ceremony. As a security precaution, there is no mention of the wedding in the newspaper.

April 23, 1998, 4:39 P.M.: Detective Mike M. has just returned to his office after making an arrest for possession of a controlled substance. There is an urgent message from Sally's new husband, John Smith. Sally did not return home from a short trip to her mother's house in a nearby city. Sally's car is later found in a parking lot, her purse still in the front seat.

May 3, 1998, 3:55 P.M.: Two hunters find the body of Sally Smith on a piece of government property near the edge of town on a chilly morning. Sally is fully clothed, and her jewelry is still on her. Sally has been strangled, the rope still around her neck. Detectives investigating the crime scene were able to make a cast of a tire track. The track was made by the kind of tire often used on off-road 4X4s and sport utility vehicles. A partial boot print was also found. One other piece of evidence almost escaped detection. As he was leaving the crime scene, detective Mike M. noticed that a small branch protruding into the path had recently been broken. He scraped minute particles of paint from the branch into a container, took pictures of the branch, and noted that the branch was broken at about 18.5 inches from the ground.

Disk Detective

May 27, 1998: You're driving to a noninjury accident investigation in an unmarked car when you spot a blue 4X4 truck parked in front of a store. The tires on the vehicle are of the type that left the imprint at the crime scene. You stop your car, jot down the license number, and investigate. Walking around, you notice a small scratch in the paint. The scratch is about 18 inches off the ground. Just as you're getting in your car to run the plates, a small man with unkempt red hair returns to the car. You follow the car for a few miles and watch as the man drives to a small farmhouse. You now have a suspect.

May 28, 1998: A judge signs a search warrant. You and two other officers execute the warrant and search the suspect's house and car for evidence. The computer is one of the items listed on the warrant. Recovering the letters would strengthen the prosecution's case against the suspect by linking him to the victim. The letters would also help establish a motive for the crime as well as premeditation.

The suspect, however, became alarmed by the car that followed him. As soon as he got home, he deleted the letters from his computer. People almost always try to destroy evidence when they think they are under suspicion. A suspect who has used a handgun to commit a murder, for example, may run a file down the barrel to change the unique markings left on the projectile. The suspect might also file down the firing pin because it too leaves a unique marking on the primer. Finally, the suspect will wipe his fingerprints and file down the serial number so that the murder weapon can't be traced to him. Yet despite all of these efforts, the firearm could still be traced back to the suspect. That's because modern investigative techniques can recover vestiges of a filed-down serial number. A similar condition exists in computer investigation. A suspect may delete information from a computer by erasing it, changing it, or formatting the disk, but that information can still be recovered.

For the purpose of demonstrating data recovery procedures, let's assume that the suspect saved and then deleted the
incriminating letters to a floppy disk. (*We use the floppy disk in
this example to guide curious readers away from practicing any data
recovery procedures on hard disks.*) To follow the suspect's steps,
we first create a fictitious letter. The letter will be saved to a
floppy disk in drive A of an IBM-compatible computer running under the Windows 3.1 and DOS 6.2. The file will be
saved under the name of *evidence.wri*.

How would the suspect delete the incriminating letters
from the floppy disk? The suspect would immediately
encounter a small hurdle in his quest to delete the file. Many
software programs do not have file delete options. Software
developers make it difficult to delete files from within programs in order to avoid the accidental or intentional deleting
of information by users. Software programs that do have
delete options often bury these options under several layers.
Our suspect, however, knows that he can delete files through
the Windows File Manager in Windows 3.1. We'll do a step-
by-step demonstration on how to delete the evidence.wri file
and then recover the deleted file. But first, let's briefly examine the role of File Manager.

File Manager is the computer's file system in Windows
3.1. The physical equivalent of File Manager is a room filled
with ordinary office file cabinets. File cabinets on the computer are called directories (or folders) and are represented
by a file folder icon (□). Sometimes the file folder icon has a
plus sign (+) inside to indicate that there are subdirectories
(or other files) within that folder. Double-clicking on the file
folder icon opens the folder (□) and displays subdirectories
or files stored within. Each directory or subdirectory can store
a number of files such as pictures, letters, accounting files,
databases or programs needed to run specific software.
Figure 1 shows a small portion of the Windows 3.1 File
Manager. Note how the selected drive (C), the selected direc-

Disk Detective

tory (windows), and the selected file (test.wri) are distinguished from other files.

Directories, subdirectories, files, and folders are selected

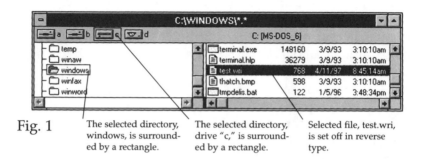

Fig. 1   The selected directory, windows, is surrounded by a rectangle.   The selected directory, drive "c," is surrounded by a rectangle.   Selected file, test.wri, is set off in reverse type.

by clicking on them with the mouse. For example, to perform an action on a file located on drive C, one clicks on the C drive icon. You know that drive C is selected because it has a small rectangle around it whereas drives A, B, and D do not. You can select a specific directory (or folder) by clicking on it as well.

When a drive, directory, or file is selected it appears different from other icons. Note that the *test.wri* file in Figure 1 has a shaded rectangle around it and the type is reversed. You can tell that the Windows directory in Figure 1 is selected because its file folder icon is shown open (🗁) whereas the icons for other directories, like Winfax, are closed (🗀) .

For the suspect to delete the *evidence.wri* file from drive A, he inserts the disk in drive A and then opens the Windows File Manager by double-clicking on the File Manager icon in the main menu of the Program Manager.

After File Manager is selected, the suspect clicks on the A drive icon. He would select the *evidence.wri* file by clicking on it. After the *evidence.wri* file is selected, he clicks on **File** (see Figure 2). From the drop-down window the suspect clicks on **Delete**, which causes the evidence file to be deleted.

> **!** Before deleting the *evidence.wri* file, File Manager issues a Confirm File Delete command: *"Delete file A:/ evidence.wri?"* After clicking <u>Y</u>es, the file is "deleted."

UNDELETING FILES IN WINDOWS 3.1

After the *evidence.wri* file is deleted, File Manager no longer shows that the *evidence.wri* file resides on drive A. The

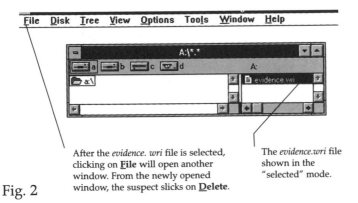

After the *evidence. wri* file is selected, clicking on **File** will open another window. From the newly opened window, the suspect slicks on **Delete**.

The *evidence.wri* file shown in the "selected" mode.

Fig. 2

suspect now assumes that the incriminating letter is deleted. That assumption is wrong! It is, in fact, easy to restore the deleted *evidence.wri* file.

There are several ways to restore deleted files using the Undelete feature found in Windows, DOS, and Norton Utilities. We begin by exploring how a file can be restored with Microsoft's Undelete feature.

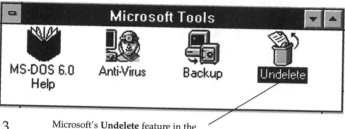

Fig. 3   Microsoft's **Undelete** feature in the
          Tools program group.

Undelete can be found in the Microsoft Tools section of the Windows Program Manager (Figure 3).

Even though File Manager did not find any files on drive A, Microsoft's Undelete finds and restores the *evidence.wri* file. To restore the *evidence.wri* file, double-click on the **Undelete** icon. This brings up Microsoft's Undelete window (Figure 4).

To recover the deleted *evidence.wri* file on drive A, click on **File** and then on **Change Drive/Directory**. After changing to drive A, Undelete displays the list of recoverable files along with a prognosis for recovery. In Figure 4, the recoverable file is called *?vidence.wri*. Note that the first letter of the file name has been replaced with a question mark. This is customary, and you will find that deleted files will be missing the first letter of their original name.

It is now a simple task to recover the *?vidence.wri* file. From the Undelete window, click on **?vidence.wri**. After clicking on **?evidence.wri**, the Undelete button in the upper left hand side of the window is highlighted. Next, click on **Undelete**. This causes a dialog box to appear prompting for the first letter of the file name. Since we know that this file was named *evidence.wri*, we type in the letter "e" and press **OK**. After replacing the first letter of the file name, Undelete displays a message that the file is being recovered.

| You do not need to know the original first letter of the file name. Simply substitute any letter for the missing letter. If, for example, we would have substituted the letter "g," the recovered file would be named *gvidence.wri.* Changing the file name to *gvidence.wri* does not change the contents of the file, only the first letter of the file name will be different.

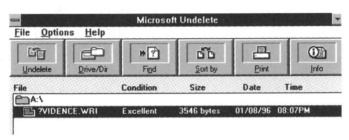

Fig. 4

Once the *evidence.wri* file is restored, close Undelete and open File Manager. File Manager will again list the *evidence.wri* file on drive A, as it did in Figure 2. The file has been successfully recovered.

UNDELETING FILES IN DOS

Undelete capabilities were packed into later versions of DOS. An easy way to determine if Undelete is available is to check the DOS manual or type **help undelete** at the DOS prompt. If Undelete is available, instructions on how to use Undelete appear.

To use DOS to recover a deleted file from a floppy disk in drive A, first change to the a drive, then type **undelete a:** at the

DOS prompt. If Undelete is available, DOS lists any recoverable files. Figure 5 shows DOS's screen dialogue after the undelete command is issued.

```
C:\>undelete a:
After typing undelete a: the following dialog appears
Undelete, a delete protection facility
Copyright (C) 1987-1993 Central Point Software, Inc.
All rights reserved
Directory A:\
File specifications: *.*
Delete Sentry control file not found
Deletion Tracking control file not found
MS-DOS directory contains 1 deleted file
Of those ! files may be recovered.
Using the MS-DOS directory method
?VIDENCE.WRI  3456  01--8-96  8:07p  ...AUndelete (Y/N)?
Please type in the first character foe the ?vidence.wri:
(After typing in a E [for the first letter of the file, press Enter] DOS issues
the following message)
File successfully undeleted.
```

Fig. 5

DOS indicates that the Delete Sentry and Deletion Tracking files could not be found. This is DOS's way to let you know that advanced undelete protection capabilities have not been set up.

To determine the level of undelete protection set up in DOS, type **Undelete** at the DOS prompt. DOS will prompt you if it does not find the Delete Sentry or Delete Tracking file. This, of course, means that these higher levels of protection are not configured. In our example, only the delete Standard was on guard. As we saw, however, delete Standard still allowed for the recovery of the deleted file.

The three levels of protection that can be configured in DOS are Delete Sentry, Delete Tracker, and Standard. Of these three methods, Delete Sentry offers the greatest chance for future file recovery.

1. **Delete Sentry** sets up a hidden directory for deleted files. When a file is deleted, Delete Sentry places the deleted file in this hidden directory.
2. **Delete Tracker** offers a lesser degree of file recovery. Rather than placing the file in a special directory, Delete Tracker simply remembers where the deleted file was located.
3. **Standard** undelete protection can still recover files, provided that the files have not been overwritten.

! **You cannot recover more files by selecting a higher level of undelete protection after the fact (i.e., after files have already been deleted). Setting a higher level of undelete protection increases future file recovery prospects.**

CONFIGURING UNDELETE PROTECTION

Undelete for Windows 3.x can be configured with three levels of protection. Setting a higher level of protection increases information recovery prospects for files deleted in the future. To determine which level of undelete protection is selected, double-click on **Microsoft Undelete** (see Figure 4) and then click on **O**ptions.

To modify the level of undelete protection in Windows 3.1, go to **Microsoft Tools** and then click on the **Undelete** icon. From the next window click on **O**ptions. From the drop-down window click on **Configure Delete Protection**. A window appears prompting the user to select a level of delete protection. If you choose Delete Tracker, you will be asked to select the drive you want

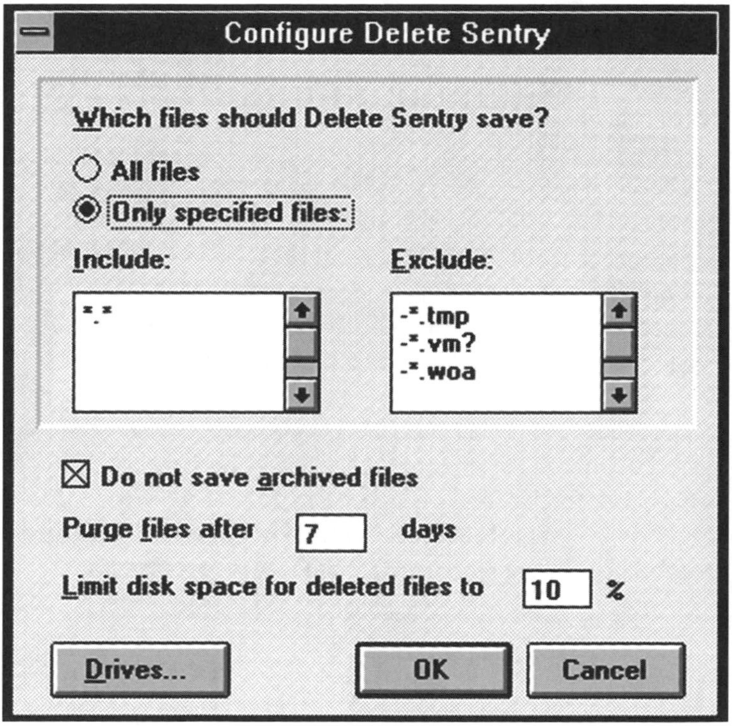

Configure Delete Sentry

W̲hich files should Delete Sentry save?

○ All files

◉ Only specified files:

I̲nclude: E̲xclude:

.		-*.tmp
		-*.vm?
		-*.woa

☒ Do not save a̲rchived files

Purge f̲iles after   `7`   days

L̲imit disk space for deleted files to   `10`   %

[D̲rives...]   [**OK**]   [**Cancel**]

Fig. 6

Tracker to protect. After the computer is rebooted, Tracker will be on guard.

If you opt for Delete Sentry you need to define specific parameters such as how many days to wait till the computer purges the protected file and how much disk space to apportion to these saved files (see Figure 6).

After rebooting the computer, the new level of protection will be in effect. Keep in mind that the more advanced undelete features are memory-resident and will take up memory as well as disk space.

> **❗** The level of Undelete protection can also be configured
> through DOS. For instructions about how to configure
> **●** this feature, type help undelete at the DOS prompt or
> refer to your manual.

UNDELETING WITH NORTON UTILITIES

DOS and Windows are not the only programs that can
recover deleted files. Norton Utilities includes similar, but
even more advanced, recovery features. To restore an erased
file from a floppy disk, for example, we place the disk into the
drive bay of a computer that has Norton Utilities 8.0 installed.

Start Norton Utilities by typing **Norton** at the DOS
prompt. Select **UnErase** from the Recovery menu (see Figure
7). Norton prompts for the drive that contains the erased
file(s). Look for this prompt near the bottom of the screen. At
the prompt, type the letter "a" followed by a colon (i.e., **a:**)
and then press **Enter**. Norton's file recovery menu appears
with three selections: Info, View, and UnErase.

- **Info** option displays a file recovery prognosis as well as
  time, date, and file size information.
- **View** option lets you view the contents of the file.
- **UnErase** option prompts for the first letter of the file and
  gives you the size of the file as well as the file's date and
  time information. After the first letter is entered, Norton
  recovers the deleted file.

You can also recover deleted files from a computer's
hard disk even if Norton Utilities is not installed on that
computer. For example, to unerase a file stored on a hard
disk, first change to the directory that contains the erased
file. For example, if the deleted file was created using the

Disk Detective

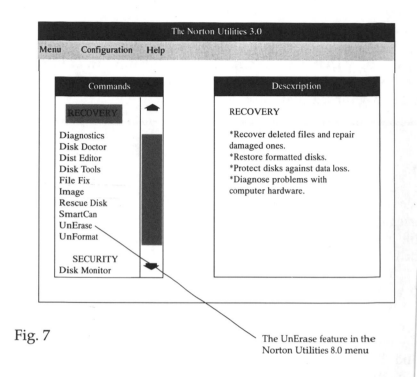

Fig. 7

The UnErase feature in the
Norton Utilities 8.0 menu

Windows Write program, change to the Windows directory
To make Windows the active directory, type **cd windows** a
the C:\> prompt and press **Enter**. The DOS screen nov
reads C:\ WINDOWS>.

Next, place the Norton Utilities Emergency/Data Recovery
Disk in drive A. Type **a:unerase** and press **Enter**. Norton then
displays a list of recoverable files and provides a prognosis for
their recovery. Select the file(s) you want to unerase by using
the up and down arrows. Then press the **Alt** key and, with the
Alt key still depressed, press the letter "u," or use the mouse to
click on **UnErase**. UnErase prompts for the first letter of the
file. Enter the first letter of the file name if you know it. If you
don't know the first letter, enter any letter. UnErase then
restores the erased file(s) and shows them as being recovered.

Exploring the Data Deletion Myth

The Windows 95 Recycle Bin makes it easy to retrieve deleted information. Double-clicking on the Recycle Bin displays a list of deleted files that can be restored. To recover a file in the Recycle Bin, simply highlight the file and then select File/Restore. This causes Windows 95 to restore files back to their original location. Be sure you note the name and location of the file(s) before you restore them, otherwise you may have difficulty locating them.

Files deleted in Windows 95 are sent to the Recycle Bin. The Windows Recycle Bin does not keep track of all deleted files, however. Files erased through specific software programs, deleted from floppy disks, or deleted through DOS can escape Recycle Bin protection.

Norton Utilities 2.0 for Windows 95 includes an UnErase Wizard that can increase file recovery prospects even for files not protected by the Recycle Bin. Unerase Wizard helps preserve and recover overwritten files. **NOTE:** Do not install data recovery programs or other software on a computer thought to contain recoverable information. Installing any kind of software could overwrite recoverable information, such as deleted files and information in slack areas.

Notice!

Deleted files or fragments of files can be recovered! Permanently "erasing" confidential information can be accomplished with special programs, such as the Wipe feature found in some versions of Norton Utilities, micro zap software, or certain shareware programs. A wipe overwrites the selected file or unused disk area with specific characters, such as zeros. Wipe features vary by software versions; consult specific software manuals for more information.

This chapter served as an introduction to basic file recovery procedures and capabilities. Recovering deleted files can be an important factor for law enforcement officers and private investigators who may be able to find valuable information in these deleted files. Suppose someone embezzles $1,000,000 from his employer before vanishing. Clues to the suspect's whereabouts may well be found in his most recently deleted files. He may have corresponded with a conspirator or accomplice about their getaway plans. This information can narrow the search and help nab the suspect and recover the stolen funds. Children who run away or are lured away may also leave clues in previously deleted files.

The most important lesson of this chapter is that deleted files can often be recovered. We have also introduced basic file recovery techniques, including recovery utilities that are found in Norton Utilities, Windows 3.x, DOS, and the Windows 95 Recycle Bin.

The next chapter will delve briefly into data recovery theory to provide a better insight into why deleted information can be recovered.

Chapter Two

Introduction to Data Recovery

The reasons that "erased" information can be recovered is not as mysterious as it sounds. In fact, the principle that allows for the recovery of files is really quite simple. Operating systems, such as recent versions of DOS and Windows, do not actually erase files at all. The process of actually "erasing" a file would take lots of time because the operating system would have to replace every character of that file with another character. Since everyone wants computers to be fast, the operating system dispenses with replacing characters. The result is that operating systems do not really erase files. If you have ever "erased" a huge file, you probably noticed that it takes just a second or two to "erase." This process is so fast because the file is not being erased at all.

Instead of erasing (or overwriting) data, many operating systems make a quick internal bookkeeping notation. This consists of changing the first letter of the file name. The operating system then marks the space previously occupied by that file as being available. Figure 8 is a simplified schematic that shows how a computer handles deleted files. Note that the *evidence.wri* file is stored in clusters 241 and 242. After this file is deleted, the bookkeeping system considers clusters 241 and 242 to be available even though the information from the deleted *evidence.wri* file remains entirely intact!

	File Name	File Location on Disk	File Location on Disk
Before Deleting File	evidence.wri	Cluster 241 contains evidence.wri file	Cluster 242 contains evidence.wri file
After Deleting File	Invalid file name (?vidence.wri) Cluster 241 & 242 are available	evidence.wri file data is still located in Cluster 241!	evidence.wri file data is still located in Cluster 242

Fig. 8

As you can see, deleting a file does not really delete any of the file's contents. Deleting a file only notifies the operating system that the space occupied by that file is available for use by another file.

This situation is analogous to a conference room that has been rented by a business group from 8:00 A.M. to noon. Let's say that this business group stays beyond the allotted time. The secretary who keeps the room calendar gets a call at 12:15 P.M. requesting the room for 1:00 P.M. Her calendar shows that the conference room is available, even though it is in fact still occupied. It is only when the second group arrives that the first group is asked to leave and will, in fact, vacate the room.

Figure 9 shows a situation where even though a portion of a deleted file is overwritten, some parts of the original file can still be recovered.

Note in Figure 9 that even after a new file is written to cluster 241, a portion of the information from the original *evidence.wri* file continues to reside in cluster 242. This portion of the erased file can still be recovered using advanced recovery procedures outlined in subsequent chapters.

The reason that the recovery of such information is possible is because the computer allocates a minimal amount of disk

	File Name	File Location on Disk	File Location on Disk
Before Deleting File	evidence.wri	Cluster 241 contains evidence.wri file	Cluster 242 contains evidence.wri file
After Deleting File	Invalid file name (?vidence.wri) Cluster 241 & 242 are available	evidence.wri file data is still located in Cluster 241!	evidence.wri file data is still located in Cluster 242
New File	new.wri	new.wri file now occupies all of Cluster 241	part of evidence.wri information is still located in Cluster 242

Fig. 9

area to a file no matter what the file's size. This area is some-times known as a cluster or an allocation unit. When you save a file that is only one word long, the computer still allocates one complete cluster to that file, resulting in lots of slack space. It writes the single word and some file information to the disk and then places an end-of-file marker in the cluster. If this cluster contained previous information, a portion of that information can still be recovered. Figure 10 represents a situation where a file named *new.wri* is written to cluster 241. Remember, cluster 241 previously contained the *evidence.wri* file. The *new.wri* file, however, does not take up the entire cluster; let's assume it needs just half of cluster 241. What happens is that *new.wri* takes up as much space as it needs. The operating system then places an end-of-file marker at the end of the *new.wri* file. What happens to the remainder of the *evidence.wri* file? The portion of the *evidence.wri* file that was not overwritten can still be recovered. The portion of the cluster that is not used by the new file is known as slack space or cluster overhang. Whatever information resides in slack space can be recovered. That's why it is so difficult to delete information from a computer disk. Slack space may hold key information for the investiga-

Disk Detective

	File Name	File Location on Disk	File Location on Disk
Before Deleting File	evidence.wri	Cluster 241 contains evidence.wri file	Cluster 242 contains evidence.wri file
After Deleting File	Invalid file name (?vidence.wri) Cluster 241 & 242 are available	evidence.wri file data is still located in Cluster 241!	evidence.wri file data is still located in Cluster 242
New File	new.wri	new.wri file is now located here / part of evidence.wri file is still here	part of evidence.wri information is still located in Cluster 242

Fig. 10

tor, information that continues to reside on the disk unbeknownst to the computer user.

Figure 10 shows what happens when a new, smaller file overwrites a deleted file. Note that the new.wri file takes up just half of cluster 241. But the other half of cluster 241 is still occupied by part of the original *evidence.wri* file. Therefore, information from the original file can still be recovered. The ability of disks to retain deleted information is one reason why it is virtually impossible for individuals to know what vestiges of information continue to reside on their hard or floppy disks.

Windows 95 stores deleted files in the Recycle Bin. Files in the the Recycle Bin can be easily recovered by clicking on the Recycle Bin icon and selecting the file(s) for restoration. The selected files are then restored to their original locations.

Files deleted (or emptied) form the Recycle Bin can still be recovered! Doing so requires knowing the file name and the folder or subfolder where the file resided. Some detective work may enable the searcher to find the names of these files and their locations and to reconstruct the file names. The process of restoring deleted Recycle Bin files involves copying the UNDELETE.EXE command found in DOS 6.x to the COMMAND subfolder of the main Windows 95 Folder. Then, Windows 95 needs to be restarted in DOS mode. Next, one has to change to the folder that contained the deleted file. After you type **lock** and press ENTER, Windows prompts for a yes or no to be sure that direct disk access is wanted. Next, one would type **undelete** followed by the name of the file (e.g., **undelete** *filename*). The next screen will look virtually identical to Figure 5 in Chapter 1. Following the screen prompts will result in undeleting these files. The final step after undeleting from the Recycle Bin is to disable the direct disk access by typing **unlock**. This entire procedure, like other examples in this book, should only be performed by a trained data recovery expert.

Note that we have been primarily dealing with recovering text from a deleted file. Other files like graphics or sound files might be virtually impossible to recover, even by trained data recovery experts, when portions of these files have been overwritten.

The next chapter details how to recover information from a formatted disk. We will once again refer to the fictitious murder case of Sally G.

In the first two chapters we discussed how deleted files can be restored and the basic framework that makes information recovery possible. In the next chapter we discuss how files deleted by the process of formatting the disk can be recovered.

Chapter Three

Recovering from Format

In Chapter 1, we observed as a fictional suspect tried to delete an incriminating letter from a floppy disk. We demonstrated how this letter was deleted and then recovered. In this chapter we follow the suspect as he tries to delete the incriminating letter by formatting the disk.

! ● Caution: Never unformat a floppy disk or a hard disk that contains, or may contain, useful information. Unformatting may permanently overwrite or delete information stored on the disk

Computer disks must be formatted before they can be used by the operating system. Formatting divides the disk into sectors that are managed by the operating system. Years ago, there were no preformatted disks. If you purchased a box of floppies, you would have to format each disk before it could be used. Disks can be formatted in both DOS and Windows. If you have ever formatted a disk, you know that Windows issues a stern warning before beginning the format (see Figure 11).

Confirm Format Disk

Formatting will erase ALL data from your disk. Are you sure that you want to format the disk in drive A?

| Yes | No |

Fig. 11

Despite this stern warning, formatting a disk is no guarantee that the files and information stored on that disk will be permanently erased. Whether formatting actually overwrites existing information depends on several factors, including the version of DOS that was used to format the disk and which switches were used with the DOS format command.

Earlier versions of DOS did overwrite information during the format process. As DOS evolved, however, programmers added additional speed and safety features to the format process. DOS versions of 5.0 and later made it possible to recover information from a formatted disk. Today, few computers operate on DOS versions earlier than 5.0, and the suspect in Sally's murder would be mistaken if he thought formatting was a surefire way to delete the incriminating letters.

Before we outline the unformat process, let's look at how the suspect in Sally G.'s murder might have formatted his floppy disk with the intent to delete evidence. First, the floppy containing the Sally G. letter is placed in drive A. After starting File Manager, he selects drive A by clicking on the icon for drive A. He then clicks on **Disk** (Figure 12). Clicking on **Disk** opens a drop-down window. From the drop-down window, he clicks on **Format Disk**. Before formatting the disk, File Manager warns that formatting erases all data from the disk. File Manager also asks for a format confirmation

Recovering from Format

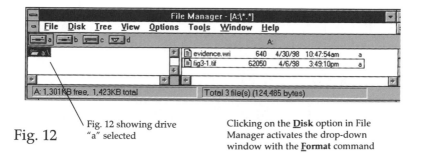

Fig. 12

Fig. 12 showing drive "a" selected

Clicking on the **Disk** option in File Manager activates the drop-down window with the **Format** command

(see Figure 11). After **Yes** is clicked, the disk is formatted.

Formatting in Windows 95 can be done by right clicking a drive icon or through Winfile in much the same manner as it is in Windows 3.1. The only difference is that in Windows 95 one must first find the Winfile directory. Since we will be referring to Winfile in subsequent chapters, we will outline how to find the Winfile folder.

1. From Windows 95, click on **Start**.
2. Move the pointer to **Programs**.
3. When the program window opens, move the mouse to Windows Explorer and click on **Explorer**.
4. Scroll down the list of folders in the left-hand window until you reach the **Windows** folder.
5. Click on the **Windows** folder.
6. Using the scroll bar on the right side, scroll down till the **Winfile** application appears.
7. Double-click on **Winfile**. This opens the File Manager that Windows 3.x users recognize.
8. Click on the **Disk** option on the menu bar.
9. From the drop-down window, select **Format Disk**.

FORMATTING WITH DOS

At the DOS prompt, type **format** followed by the letter of the drive that contains the disk to be formatted. To format a disk on a computer with drive A designated as a floppy drive, type **format a:**. After entering the format command, DOS prompts for the disk to be inserted into the A drive. DOS then prompts the user to strike the **ENTER** key.

UNFORMATTING WITH DOS

Now that you understand the formatting process, let's take a step-by-step look at how to unformat a disk and restore information it contained. The computer we are using in this example is a 486 running Windows 3.1 and DOS 6.2. Insert the floppy disk into disk drive A. At the DOS prompt, change to the DOS directory by typing **cd DOS**. Then, type **unformat a:** (i.e., the letter **a** followed by a colon). Figure 13 shows DOS's dialogue after the unformat command.

The degree of success Unformat has in restoring a disk depends on how the disk was formatted and which switches were used with the format command. Later versions of DOS checked for files remaining on the disk. If files are found, DOS takes a snapshot of the disk's boot sector, the root directory, and the file allocation table. DOS stores this snapshot on a normally unused area of the disk. Then, when the Unformat command is issued, DOS searches for the snapshot information and uses this information to restore the disk to its preformatted condition. After entering the unformat command, DOS issues several warnings and messages (see Figure 13).

Unformat does not come with a 100 percent guarantee for recovering information. Unformat may have difficulty restoring fragmented files from hard disks. DOS also offers some help to determine if Unformat can restore a formatted disk. To learn more about Unformat, type **help unformat** at the DOS prompt and press **Enter**.

DOS has two important utilities that can be used to determine if a disk should be unformatted. To access these

*To unformat a formatted disk, type **unformat**, followed by the letter of the drive that contains the disk you wish to unformat. Thus, the command to unformat a floppy disk in drive a is **unformat a:***

    C:\>unformat a:
Dos issues the following command:
        insert disk to rebuild in drive A:
        and press ENTER when ready.
After inserting the disk and pressing enter, DOS issues a warning:
        Restores the system area of your disk by using the image file created by the
        MIRROR command.

        WARNING!! WARNING!!
        This command should be used to recover from the inadvertent use of the
        FORMAT command or RECOVER command. Any other use of the
        UNFORMAT d command may cause you to lose data! Files modified since
        the MIRROR Image file was last created may be lost.

        Searching disk for MIRROR image.
        The last time the MIRROR or FORMAT command was used was at 06;47
        ON 06-05-98
        The MIRROR image file has been validated.
        Are you sure you want to update the system area of your drive A (Y/N)

After pressing Y, DOS unformats the disk and validates its work

        The system area of drive A has been rebuilt.
        You may need to restart the system.

Fig. 13

utilities, first change to the DOS directory by typing **cd DOS** at the C:\> prompt. Next, type **unformat a: /test** and press **Enter**. DOS then conducts a search and prompts you again before anything is altered. A second utility lists the files and subdirectories stored on a previously formatted disk. This list can be obtained by typing **unformat a: /l** at the DOS prompt.

UNFORMATTING WITH NORTON UTILITIES

! Norton Utilities can also unformat disks. Norton's
● UnFormat command cannot recover floppy disks format-
ted with DOS versions of 5.0 or earlier, nor can
UnFormat recover information formatted with the /U switch.
To unformat a floppy disk using Norton Utilities, select
UnFormat from Norton's Recovery menu. Before unformat-
ting the disk, Norton lists files or subdirectories that might
be lost during the UnFormat process.

The steps to unformat a floppy disk using Norton's
UnFormat command in Norton version 8.0 on a computer
running under DOS 6.2 and Windows 3.1 are outlined below:*

1. Start the Norton Utilities program by typing **Norton** at the
    DOS prompt and press **Enter.**
2. Selected **UnFormat** from Norton's Recovery Commands
    and press **Enter.**
3. Norton issues a warning. Read the warning and, if appro-
    priate, press **Continue.**
4. From the next window, select drive A, which in our exam-
    ple is the drive that contains the floppy disk to be unfor-
    matted. Press **OK.**
5. UnFormat displays a message asking if Image or the DOS
    Mirror program was previously used. After selecting **Yes,**
    Norton lists the files located on the selected disk and dis-
    plays the following message: "Are you sure you want to
    unformat it?"
6. After selecting **Yes,** Norton searches for the Mirror or
    Image files and displays the following message: *"Restoring
    the MIRROR info to drive a: may overwrite any changes made
    to the disk since the MIRROR info was last saved. Are you
    absolutely sure you want to restore the MIRROR info to drive*

A:?" Click **Yes**, if it is appropriate to proceed.
7. Norton then offers the option of either a full or a partial restore. After selecting the **Full** restoration option, Norton starts to unformat the disk.

Norton Utilities will try to unformat the selected disk even if it cannot find the Mirror or Image file.

* **NOTE**: In the example above, Norton Utilities is installed on the hard drive.

! ● After unformatting the disk, Norton suggests that the Norton Disk Doctor be run in order to identify and correct any disk problems that may have occurred during the unformat process.

Thus far, we have restricted data recovery examples to floppy disks to discourage anyone from practicing data recovery procedure on hard disks. In the interest of understanding the data recovery process, however, we have to expand our discussions beyond the floppy.

Working with hard disks can be tricky, and even a minor mistake can damage data or wipe out the information on an entire hard drive. Consult a data recovery expert and never format or unformat a hard disk unless you are absolutely sure you know what you are doing.

Hard disks can be unformatted with a program such as the Norton Utilities version 8.0. **WARNING: DO NOT UNFORMAT A HARD DISK UNLESS YOU ARE ABSOLUTELY SURE YOU KNOW WHAT YOU ARE DOING! YOU MAY LOSE ALL EXISTING DATA ON THE HARD DISK.** The following steps outline the procedures to unformat a hard disk:

1. Boot the computer using the Norton Utilities Emergency Disk.
2. From the **Options** list, select **UnFormat** and press **Enter**.
3. A window with UnFormat information appears. After reading the information, press **Enter**.
4. After selecting the drive to unformat, press **Enter**. This brings up a number of prompts that guide the user through the recovery process.

! **There are safer ways to search for and recover information from formatted disks. These procedures will be outlined in subsequent chapters.**

A FINAL MESSAGE ABOUT UNFORMAT

Recovering information after a disk has been formatted depends on several factors, such as how the disk was used since it was last formatted, which version of DOS was used to format the disk, and which switches were used along with the format.

Adding a switch to a DOS command enables a special function that is determined by the switch. For example, Figure 14 shows the DOS format command with the added switch /u.

A:/>**format a:/u**
Syntax showing the optional /u switch which prevents subsequent unformatting of the floppy disk

Fig. 14

Data on a disk can be prevented from being recovered by using the format command with the /u switch. The /u switch tells DOS to format the disk unconditionally. This overwrites information on the disk and prevents some subsequent recovery. If the information stored on the disk is truly sensitive, however, you must use Wipe procedures.

The purpose of this chapter is to acquaint the investigator with the basic functions of unformat utilities and the fundamentals of recovery theory. Specifically, my intent was to show that formatting a disk is no guarantee against future data recovery.

In the fictitious murder case of Sally G., the suspect has thus far been unable to delete the evidence from his disk. Neither deleting the file nor formatting the disk prevented investigators from making a complete recovery of the incriminating Sally G. letters. In the next chapter we explore how to recover the Sally G. letters after the suspect has overwritten the information on the disk. We will also discover a remarkable secret about recovering information that the user never even saved at all.

Chapter Four

Advanced Search Techniques

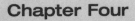

The murder of Sally G. has stirred up emotions in your town, and your department is coming under increasing pressure to arrest a suspect. The media has been following the case closely, and hardly a day goes by without this case being splashed across the front page of the newspapers. You desperately need to recover the Sally G. letters. What you don't know, however, is that the suspect is employing a clever scheme to rid his computer of the incriminating letters.

Let's assume that the suspect used the Windows 3.x Write program to draft one of the Sally G. letters.

He saved this letter under the name of evidence.wri. Let's follow our suspect as he tries to overwrite one of the Sally G. letters with other information in order to destroy the evidence.

The Write word processing program is found in the Windows Accessories group in Program Manager. After dou-

Sally G.

You havnt responded to any of my demands nor did you meet me were I told you to. I tried everything to get us together so we could talk. Then you went and got married to some scumbag. Now youre going to die bitch. Youre as good as ded.

ble-clicking on the Write icon, the suspect opens the evidence.wri file by clicking **File** and then by clicking **Open**. This brings up the Open dialogue box. The suspect then clicks on the down arrow next to the Drives dialogue box. This brings up the list of available drives. From the list of drives, he clicks on the A drive icon that represents the floppy disk drive in this example. The suspect opens the Sally G. letter file by double-clicking on **evidence.wri.**

With the evidence.wri file open the suspect changes the entire content of the letter. For example, the suspect selects all of the text in the Sally G. letter and replaces it with the Jim J. letter.

After changing the content of the letter, the suspect clicks on **File** and then clicks on **Save**. Now, whenever the evidence.wri file is opened, the new Jim J. letter appears.

Jim J.

Lets get together sometime soon. It's been a long time since................

By overwriting the entire content of the Sally G. letter, has the suspect foiled investigators or is there still a way to retrieve the incriminating original letter? Surprisingly, the original Sally G. letter can still be recovered with a utilities program, such as Norton Utilities.

Norton Utilities is a comprehensive data recovery program developed by Peter Norton. It includes a number of advanced search and recovery tools, such as the Disk Editor, that can search for key words on a hard or floppy disk.

❗ Before proceeding with search or recovery techniques using the Norton Utilities Disk Editor, follow the directions in the Norton software manual. Never install a data recovery program on the hard disk that contains information you want to recover. Installing any kind of program can overwrite information and foil subsequent recovery of this information.

We will explore two ways to uncover the information from the overwritten Sally G. letter. The first example outlines the steps to recover an overwritten text file from a floppy disk of a computer running under Windows 3.1. The second example outlines how we recovered the overwritten Sally G. letter from the hard disk on a computer running under Windows 95.

Norton Utilities provides a unique way to search for key words that may be residing on the disk. (Windows 95 also has text search features that are activated by clicking Start/Find/Files or Folders. After selecting the Advanced Tab, file in the Containing Text dialog area. What makes Norton so effective is that it can search through all the nooks and crannies on the disk to locate the key word you are looking for. In its search, Norton ferrets out information, including some that the computer user doesn't even know still exists. Some files, like those containing text, do not have to be intact for Norton to locate the key words. Let's take a step-by-step look at how to find the overwritten information from the Sally G. letter.

The following example was taken from a 486 computer with DOS 6.2, Windows 3.1, and Norton Utilities 8.0 installed. Place the floppy disk containing the overwritten Sally G. letter in drive A.

1. Type **Norton** at the DOS prompt and press **Enter**. This brings up Norton's main menu.
2. From the Recovery Commands section, select the on **Disk Editor**. This brings up the Disk Editor window and causes a blinking cursor to appear in a dialogue box at the bottom of the screen.
3. At the cursor location, type **a:** (i.e., the letter "a" followed by a colon), and then press **Enter**.

4. From the next window, click on **Object**, then click on **Drive**.

5. From Drive Options select drive A. Change the disk type from Logical disk to Physical disk by clicking on the **Physical** disk button.

6. After selecting Physical disk, click on **OK**.

7. The next screen is filled with what appears to be gibberish. To make the screen more reader friendly, click on **View** and then on **As Text**.

8. Next, click on **Tools**.

9. From the drop-down window, click on Find.

10. After clicking **Find**, a dialogue box opens and prompts for the ASCII text. Type in the text (or key word) that you want Disk Editor to find. We selected the word "youre." Thus, in the ASCII dialogue box at the top of the screen, type in the word **youre**, and then click **Find**.

Norton then begins to search through the entire disk for a text match, stopping at every reference to the selected key word. After Norton finds a match, you can use the left and right arrows to scroll to text that may be off to the side of the screen.

Key words should be carefully selected. Your key word should be one of the most uncommon words from the original document. There are several good candidates in the Sally G. letter. The word youre is excellent because it is misspelled and therefore may not generate many inaccurate hits. The word scumbag is also a good candidate because it too would not likely appear in many other documents.

Key word selection is important because the Disk Editor searches the entire disk for a text string match. Thus, entering a common word, like responded, would generate countless hits and would slow the search to a snail's pace. If you recall, the original Sally G. letter contained the misspelled word ded. Using ded as the key word may result in inaccurate hits. When we entered the word ded, Norton stopped at words like inten**ded**, which contains the text string *ded*. Choose your key words carefully. In the event of a false hit, select **Find Again** from the **Tools** menu, and the editor will search for the next text string match.

It took only about 30 seconds for Norton Utilities to find the text string youre from the overwritten letter and display the entire contents of the "overwritten" letter. Remember, though, that we searched a floppy disk. Text string searches on a hard disk can take much longer. Searching through a six-gigabyte drive might take hours.

It is normal for text displayed in Disk Editor to be surrounded by gibberish, strange characters, or disk sector information. Text editor is not a sanitized word processor that produces pretty output, but it is effective.

In the previous example we searched for a key word using the mouse. If the mouse is not active, you can use keystrokes to activate Norton's menus. In the fun and exciting world of Windows, many computer users have become unfamiliar with keystrokes, and opening the Disk Editor may throw them a curve. Therefore, the next example will find the overwritten Sally G. letter using keystrokes alone.

1. Open Norton Utilities by typing **Norton** at the DOS prompt and pressing **Enter**, which brings up Norton's main menu.
2. Push the down-arrow key till **Disk Editor** is selected. This causes a blinking cursor to appear in a dialogue box at the bottom of the screen.
3. At the cursor location, type **a:** (i.e., the letter "a" followed by a colon) and then press **Enter**.
4. When the next dialogue box appears, first press the **Alt**

Disk Detective

key. With the Alt key still depressed, press the letter "**o**." This causes a drop-down window to appear. When it does, press the **Alt** key. With the **Alt** key still depressed, press the letter "**d**."

5. The next window contains the Drive Options. Use the up or down arrows to select drive A.
6. Change the disk type from Logical disk to Physical disk by pressing the **Alt** key. With the **Alt** key still depressed, press the letter "**p**."
7. After the Physical disk is selected, press the **Alt** key. With the **Alt** key still depressed, press the letter "**o**."
8. The next screen is filled with what looks like gibberish. To make it more reader friendly press the **Alt** key. With the **Alt** key still depressed, press the letter "**v**."
9. Next, press the **Alt** key. With the **Alt** key still depressed, press the letter "**t**." Then press the **Alt** key. With the **Alt** key still depressed, press the letter "**t**." This brings up the Tools options. To select Find, press the **Alt** key. With the **Alt** key still depressed, press the letter "**f**."
10. A new dialogue box opens and prompts us to enter the ASCII text. Here we type in the text (or key word) from the original Sally G. letter that we want Disk Editor to search for. In the ASCII dialogue box at the top of the screen, we type in the word *youre* and then press the **Alt** key. With the Alt key still depressed, press the letter "**f**."

Moving around without a mouse takes some extra time and practice. Many of Norton's drop-down windows list shortcuts next to the commands. For example, a drop-down window may have the F3 symbol next to a particular command (e.g., as Text . . . F3, or Drive . . . **Alt+D**, or Mark . . . **Ctrl+B**. Such commands as F3 mean that pressing that key will activate the corresponding command. One can also use the keyboard arrows ⬆ ➡ ⬇ ⬅ to speed selections through some of the menus. When a drop-down window appears you

can use the down-arrow key to scroll to a particular command. When a particular command is highlighted, you press
the Enter key to activate the selection. To determine which letters to use with the Alt key is simple. Each option, such as
Edit, has one of its letters in bold face or a different color.
Thus, to select Edit, press the Alt key and, with the Alt key still
depressed, type in the highlighted letter. In the Edit example
that would be the letter "e" or its capitalized cousin, "E."

**Before using the Disk Editor, be absolutely certain you
know what you are doing. The default setting for
Norton's Disk Editor is Read Only. This prevents
changes being written to the disk. A slight mistake, however, may change this setting and write changes to the disk,
and portions or even the entire disk may become inoperable. Before writing any changes to the disk, Norton Utilities
offers a last-ditch opportunity to discard changes. If you've
accidentally made changes, you'll have one last opportunity
to discard them.**

We finished our exploration of how to search for overwritten information from a floppy disk. Next we will examine
how to find deleted information from a hard disk using
Norton's Disk Editor.

Because of the tremendous storage capacities of today's
hard disks, finding information on a hard disk is more chal-
lenging and time consuming than retrieving the same information from a floppy disk. Searching and finding such information is, however, not very difficult.

In previous examples, we used a 486 running under DOS
6.2 and Windows 3.1 and a computer that already had Norton
Utilities installed. Our next data recovery example will use a
computer running under Windows 95. We will use the Word

Disk Detective

Pad word processor (found in the Accessories group) to write an identical copy of the Sally G. letter. We save this letter under the name of evidence, only this time, instead of saving it to a floppy disk, we save the file to the hard disk on drive C and watch as it is recovered.

After saving the file, we restart the computer to simulate the passage of time. From the Windows 95 Start menu, we select the Word Pad program from the Accessories menu and open the *evidence* file. Once the evidence file is open we select all of the *evidence* text and delete any references to the Sally G. letter, substituting the Jim J. letter instead. We save this letter by clicking on **File** and then by clicking on **Save**. After saving the file, we shut down the computer and restart it. This time, we reopen the *evidence* file, the new Jim J. letter appears, and all previous references to the Sally G. letter are gone.

1. To recover the text from the previous Sally G. letter, turn off the computer and place the Norton Utilities Emergency Recovery Disk (disk #1) from Norton's Windows 95 version (2.0 in our example) in floppy disk drive A.
2. Turn on the computer. This causes the computer to bypass DOS and Windows and boot up instead from Norton's emergency disk. (The majority of computers will boot from a bootable disk in the A drive.) Booting from the Norton Utilities Emergency Disk brings up the Commands menu that includes the Disk Editor.
3. Use the down arrow key to select **Disk Editor** and press **Enter**.
4. Insert the Norton Utilities Emergency Disk #2 in drive A when prompted and press **Enter**. If you get a window that tells you Disk Editor is in "Read Only" mode, this is a good safety feature. Press **Enter** to proceed.
5. At the next screen, select Object by pressing the **Alt** key, and with the **Alt** key still depressed, press the letter "**o**."
6. Drive should now be highlighted. If it is not, use the up

46

and down arrows to select **Drive** and then press **Enter**.

7. Use the down arrow key to select **C: Hard Disk**. Then select Physical disk by clicking on Physical Disk or by pressing **Alt** and, with the **Alt** key still depressed, pressing the letter "**p**." Then select OK by clicking on it or by pressing **Alt** and, with the **Alt** key still depressed, press the letter "**o**."

8. Select Tools by pressing the **Alt** key and, with the **Alt** key still depressed, press the letter "**t**."

9. **Find** is now highlighted. With **Find** highlighted, press the letter "**f**." We are now ready to begin the search for the original Sally G. letter. Type in a word from the original document in the ASCII dialogue box and press **Alt** and, with the **Alt** key still depressed, press the letter "**f**."

10. Norton Utilities starts searching through the entire disk, looking for the key word. Don't expect immediate results. Searching through gigabytes of files for one text string could take some time. On my 1.2 gigabyte computer, Norton Utilities found the reference to the selected word along with all of the original Sally G. letter in about 23 minutes. That's really quite impressive when you think about it.

Text search is an extremely powerful investigative tool that can have many applications. Suppose a private investigator is working on a divorce case. The husband hires the investigator because he suspects his wife is having an affair with a guy named Franko. That's all the investigator needs to know. Using Norton Utilities, the investigator can search for any references to Franko. Norton searches through the entire disk stopping at all references to that name. Norton will find information in letters, hidden files, e-mail messages, desktop publishing programs, and just about any software program imaginable.

Suppose that the husband does not know the other man's name. Even then, the investigator can search the computer for specific terms of endearment such as sweetheart, honey, love, darling, or the like. Law enforcement officers can use the same principle to search for key words or a word relating to a victim or crime by searching for the victim's name, etc.

The length of time that information remains on a disk depends on a number of factors, including how much disk space is available and how much information has been written to the disk since the original information was deleted or modified. Information can be overwritten the next day, or it can remain on the computer for many years. Time, however, is of the essence, so get the computer as quickly as possible.

One can speed up key word searches by looking in specific directories. Let's take the case of an underage teen who ran away with a soldier named Bonko. Suppose the parents know that the girl usually writes to her friend using the Word Pad word processing program. This information allows the investigator to streamline his search by limiting it to (or at least starting in) the Word Pad directory. Instead of searching the entire disk, the investigator selects the specific directory (folder) that is thought to contain the information. (Instead of searching through the entire hard disk for references to Bonko, the investigator limit his search to the Word Pad folder.)

After finishing the search, exit Disk Editor by following the instructions in the manual. Usually this means pressing the **Alt** key and, with the **Alt** key still depressed, pressing the letter "**o**." From the next drop-down window press **x**. Remove the Emergency Disk #2 from drive A, insert Emergency Disk #1 when prompted, and press any key. At the next prompt, remove Emergency Disk #1 and reboot the computer by simultaneously pressing **Ctrl + Alt + Delete**.

The more faint at heart can also search for specific text without using the Editor. Norton has a Text Search option that is found in Norton Utilities' Tools section. Text Search will search for particular text strings, such as ded or scumbag. The text can be displayed or written to a file. Norton's Text Search is more limited than Disk Editor, but it is also easier to use and there is less chance for making an inadvertent change to the disk. Later versions of DOS also included a "find" feature that helps locate specific text strings. To determine if you have DOS's Find available, consult your DOS manual or type **help find** at the DOS prompt and press Enter.

The preceding example can also be performed on Windows 3.1. With the appropriate software you do not have to have Norton installed to conduct a text search. Consult your Norton manual for complete details. Norton Utilities includes more advanced data recovery methods that can search for files stored in noncontiguous clusters. In other words, these are files that exceed one cluster in size where the next cluster may be located on a nonadjacent part of the disk. This feature can help restore entire files. This feature can also be used to reconstruct graphics files, such as those containing pictures, databases, spreadsheets, etc. Remember, text files are easy to find and interpret. Other files, such as graphic files, will likely need to be reconstructed from all clusters before they can be opened. Text written in these files can, however, be simple to recover with the procedures outlined above. For complete information, consult the Norton Utilities manual.

Some programs, like Word, have autosave features designed to protect the user from losing the information because of power failures or general protection faults, etc. Autosave works by saving an open file at regular intervals, usually every 5 or 10 minutes. What happens, then, if an individual types a document, prints it out, but never saves that document to a disk? Because the autosave feature is activated, such a document can be recovered with a program such as Norton Utilities. Thus, even though a suspect never saves information to a disk, that information can, in some instances, still be recovered. Other Windows 95 features save information automatically. Thus, there are lots of opportunities to find information. Be sure to check the Windows Temp folder. You may find all kinds of information there.

We have covered a lot of information in this chapter. The next chapter will provide an overview of how to retrace visited Internet Web sites to find out where and when computer users logged on to these sites.

Chapter Five

Retracing Visited Internet Sites

In the 1980s, emergency medical technicians (EMTs) were called to a mobile home in the Pacific Northwest. When they arrived, they found an unconscious, middle-aged man writhing on the floor. The man's pulse was erratic, his face flushed. The EMTs rushed the man to the hospital, where he died a short time later. He was listed as having died of natural causes. Officials became suspicious, however, after the man's wife repeatedly questioned the official cause of death. An autopsy was performed, and, sure enough, the medical examiner found cyanide in the victim's body. The cause of death was revised and a criminal investigation launched.

The investigation focused on the victim's wife who, it was discovered, had taken out a large life insurance policy on her husband. The policy had a larger payout for an accidental death, as in an alleged product-tampering case. Investigators received an unexpected lead that the suspect spent many hours at the library. Investigators questioned librarians about the kind of books the suspect had been reading. Investigators soon learned that the suspect had a keen interest in books about poisons. They seized scores of books and sent them to the FBI for fingerprint analysis. When the results came back, authorities had the evidence needed to get a conviction. The FBI found over 100 of the suspect's fingerprints and several palm prints on books about poison. The fingerprints, along with other evidence, led to a conviction and a life sentence.

That same case today would have to be handled entirely different, because for a growing number of Internet-literate individuals the library is as obsolete at the Pony Express. If you want to find information on poisons or cyanide, you don't have to leave the comfort of your very own home. Nor do you have to leave fingerprints on library books. Today, you can type the word cyanide into one of the Internet's many search engines and within moments, you'll have more information about cyanide at your fingertips than at any public library in the world.

The information on the Internet is growing exponentially, and so are the number of people who use the Internet. How can an investigator determine if a suspect has been visiting sites about poisoning, or any sites for that matter? Surprisingly, computers often reveal not only what sites were visited but also on what date and at what time.

Retracing visited Internet sites can be an important and enlightening source of information for investigators, law enforcement officers, teachers, or the parents of a runaway child. People who surf the Internet leave traces of their online activities on the computer. An investigator who knows how to retrace visited Internet sites can uncover valuable leads that can be useful in a variety of law enforcement and private investigative applications.

To retrace Internet sites, we need to return to our old friends, the File Manager and the Windows Explorer. If you recall, these are the file management systems that act

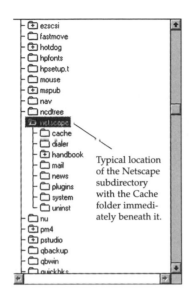

Typical location of the Netscape subdirectory with the Cache folder immediately beneath it.

Fig. 15

as common gateways to finding information that is stored on computers.

Windows 95 users who are more comfortable with File Manager can open the old-style File Manager by clicking on **Windows Explorer**, then clicking on the **Windows** folder, and then scrolling down to the **Winfile** program. Winfile is identified by the small file cabinet icon that precedes it. Double-clicking on Winfile opens the old-style File Manager (see Figure 15).

Once File Manager or Explorer is open, you need to find the file folder for the Internet browser, e.g., Netscape, Internet Explorer, Mosaic, etc. The most likely browser will be Netscape, one of today's most popular browsers. Figure 15 shows the typical location of the Netscape directory in File Manager of Windows 3.1. You can find the location of Netscape in Windows 95 by clicking on **Start** and then clicking on **Find**. Next, click on Files or **Folders**. In the dialogue box, type the word **Netscape** then click **Find Now**. From the list of files, look for the Netscape File Folder and double-click on it. A new window appears with the **Navigator** folder. Double-click on **Navigator**. Look for the cache folder and double-click on **Cache**. You can also find the cache folder in the Windows Explorer.

Cache folders, like those found in Netscape, hold the key to retracing visited Internet sites. That's because Cache retains information including pictures, URLs (Internet addresses), and other information. Cache is really designed to provide faster Internet response by keeping certain information in the computer's file system. Many people visit the same site over and over or go back to previously visited sites in the same online session. When they do, the computer loads information from Cache rather than going through the process of retrieving information from a faraway server. That's the real reason for Cache, not to help investigators, parents, or teachers.

Individuals who access the Internet through an online service may have a separate folder for their browser, as Netscape does. In America Online, for example, the cache folder will be located in the America Online Directory, which may be named aol30 or something similar. Other times cache folders can be found in temporary Internet folders.

Our first example of how to retrace visited Internet sites uses the Netscape Navigator 2.0 and 3.0 browser. Clicking on the Netscape file folder icon (Figure 15) displays the Netscape subdirectories, including the cache folder. Opening the cache folder is like opening a treasure trove of information about previously visited Internet sites. An investigator can discover which sites were visited as well as when these files were last modified.

Figure 16 shows some of files from an earlier America

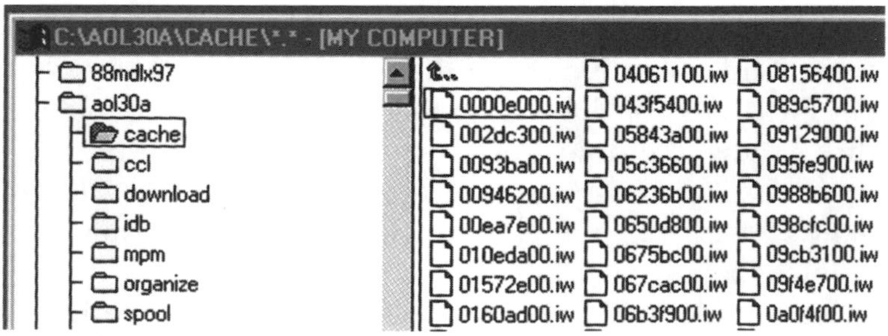

Fig. 16

Online cache as they appear in the Windows 95 Winfile folder. Note that the cache file folder icon is shown open. The window on the right shows cache files beginning with file 0000e000.iw.

Cache files can often be opened by simply double-clicking on them. Other times, however, you may have to associate (called "open with" in Windows 95) a cache file before it opens. Associating files is discussed later in this chapter, but it is best to consult your operating system manual for complete details.

If a file opens by double-clicking on it, as most will, the investigator's job is easy. All he, or she, has to do is double-click on one of the files, and a page from the visited Internet site or a picture from this site appears. Sometimes even URL addresses and other useful information are displayed. Here is a step-by-step outline of how to open a Netscape 3.0 Cache file in Windows 95.

1. Move the pointer to **Start** and click once.
2. Move the pointer to **Programs**.
3. Move the pointer to **Windows Explorer** and click once.
4. Find the Netscape folder (if you don't find Netscape here, skip this section and follow the steps in the next example).
5. Move the pointer to the **Netscape** folder and click once.
6. Find the Cache folder (look at the top of the window on the right side of the screen).
7. Double-click on **Cache**.
8. The Cache files should now appear on the right-side window.
9. In a computer that has been used to surf the Internet, this brings up a list of Moq files including GIF images, JPEG images, and Netscape Hypertext documents along with file type, file size, and the date and time the individual files were modified.
10. Pick one of the Moq files and double-click on it. If you select a GIF or JPEG file, your default graphics program will open, and you will likely see a picture from one of the visited

sites. If you select a Netscape Hypertext Document, your default browser will open, and you can get a near full page from a visited Internet site. Hypertext areas in the displayed text may even be active, and moving the pointer over a hypertext area can reveal the actual URL or E-mail address from the visited site. Look near the bottom of the screen (right above the Start button) for these hypertext links. Sometimes moving the pointer over the hypertext areas only reveals internal computer information. Such internal information is usually preceded by the word "file."

(If you experience difficulties opening a file, see the section about associating files and other tactics later in this chapter.)

To select another Cache folder for viewing, click on File and then click on Close. This takes you back to the Cache folder. If you could not locate the Netscape folder as per the previous example, try looking in the Program Files folder using the following steps:

1. Move the pointer to **Start** and click once.
2. Move the pointer to **Programs**.
3. Move the pointer to **Windows Explorer** and click once.
4. Find the Program Files folder.
5. Move the pointer to **Program Files** and click once.
6. Find the Netscape folder (look near the middle of the folders on the right-side window).
7. Move the pointer to the **Netscape** folder and double-click on **Netscape**.
8. The Navigator folder should appear in the right-side window.
9. Double-click on the **Navigator** folder.
10. The Cache folder should now appear at the top of the right-side window.
11. Double-click on **Cache**. In a computer that has been used to surf the Internet, this brings up a list of Moq files, including GIF images, JPEG images, and

Netscape Hypertext Documents. The window also displays file type, file size, and the date and time the file was modified.

12. Pick one of the Moq files and double-click on it. If you select a GIF or JPEG file, you may get a picture from one of the visited sites. If you select one of the Netscape Hypertext Documents, you can get a full page of a visited Internet site. Hypertext areas can be active, and moving the pointer over a hypertext area can reveal the actual URL, e-mail address, etc. You'll need to look near the bottom of the screen (right above the Start button) for addresses. Other times, the hypertext will only reveal internal computer information (internal documents are usually preceded by the word "file").

13. To select another cache folder for viewing, click on **File** and then click on **Close**. This takes you back to the cache folder.

In some instances, double-clicking on a file folder will not open the program, but will instead generate an error message such as:

**Cannot Run Program — No application
is associated with this file.**

**Choose associate from the File menu
to create an association.**

If this should happen, you must first associate the file(s) in the cache subdirectory with a suitable program. The following steps can be used to associate a file in Windows 3.1, but always refer to your operating manual for complete details.

1. Click on one of the files. For example, to associate the

Disk Detective

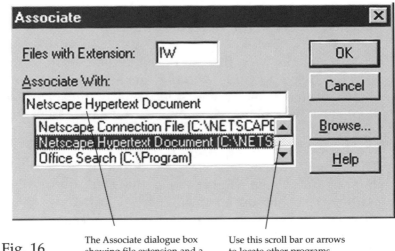

Fig. 16

The Associate dialogue box showing file extension and a list of program associations. Note that files with iw are associated with "none."

Use this scroll bar or arrows to locate other programs.

cache files, click on one of the files, such as 0000-e000.iw file in Figure 16.
2. Click on **File**. This causes a drop down window to appear
3. From the list of options in the window click on **Associate** box.
4. The next window displays a message such as "Files with Extension [iw] Associate with." From the associate window use the scroll bars to select a program to open the file. If you need help in determining which program to select, press the **Help** button or consult your Windows manual.

Fig. 17   An "Open With" window used to associate files in Windows 95. Check
           here if you want to always use your selected program to open this
           type of file. My preference is to leave this area unchecked.

Name	Size	Type	Modified
01807e00	3KB	IW File	6/1/97 6:22 PM
02b9e000	1KB	IW File	6/3/97 5:21 PM
02c02a00	1KB	IW File	6/4/97 2:53 PM
02dfce00	5KB	IW File	6/4/97 3:01 PM
031b2c00	7KB	IW File	6/4/97 3:29 PM
031c3d00	7KB	IW File	6/4/97 3:06 PM
03bca200	2KB	IW File	6/4/97 3:20 PM
04061100	4KB	IW File	5/26/97 11:05 AM

Fig. 18

After associating a file, it is probably a good idea to reassociate it with the original program (see your operating system manual for more details).

Some cache files may not contain useful information, but others will. If a certain file does not yield anything of value, move on to the next file in the series until you discover something useful.

Opening a cache file may display a page from a visited Internet site. Moving the mouse pointer to the colored hypertext of such a displayed file may cause the URL to be displayed in the lower left corner of the screen. Once the URL is identified, the investigator can write it down and use that address to visit the actual site, preferably from another computer. For example, a private investigator could discover that a runaway teen had repeatedly visited the Web site of a bizarre religious cult. The investigator could log on to the cult's site from another computer and discover valuable information such as recruiting techniques, and, most importantly, cult locations. This information could then be used to find the teen.

Retracing Visited Internet Sites

! ● Avoid using the computer that is being investigated to visit Internet sites. What happens is that the sites visited by the investigator end up in Cache. Since Cache may have limited space allotted to it, other Cache files will be forced out, and the information they contain could be lost or more difficult to retrieve.

Newer browsers and online services have made finding cache files a bit more difficult. Sometimes cache files can be found in a file folder named Temporary Internet. This folder can have several cache folders identified as cache1, cache2, cache3, etc. The problem is that these temporary Internet and cache folders may have the hidden attribute set, making them invisible to a standard configuration of the Explorer. The good news is that the newer expanded cache folders contain much more detailed information about visited Web sites. Here is an easy way to find cache folders and open them up, even if they have the hidden attribute set:

1. Click on **Start**.
2. Move the pointer to **Find**.
3. Move the pointer to **Files or Folders** and click.
4. In the dialogue box, type in the word **cache** and click on **Find Now**.
5. Look for cache folders that are preceded by a yellow file folder icon (there could be several cache folders named cache1, cache2, cache3, cache4) These folders may be located in the C:\Windows\Temp or C:\Windows\Temporary\Internet folder or in a browser folder like Netscape.
6. Choose a folder and double-click on it. This should cause the contents of the cache file to appear.

Disk Detective

Because of the different software and browser configurations/versions, it may take a bit of detective work to locate the cache folders. But when they are found, they can reveal important information about the interests of the computer user. Remember that individuals can set preferences in their browser settings. These settings can impact the information in Cache.

Cache can be a vital source of information about visited Internet sites, but there are additional ways to discover information about someone's Internet browsing habits.

Online services and Web browsers usually have a Favorite Places or Bookmarks sections. Favorite Places and Bookmarks are like speed dialers on a telephone that allow you to program in your office telephone number or some other frequently called number. Then, by pressing just one button, your call is dialed and connected to the appropriate number.

Because Internet addresses can be extremely lengthy and difficult to remember, browsers include the equivalent of speed dialers for Internet addresses. You can find these speed-dial Internet addresses in any number of ways. From the main America Online screen, click on **Go To** and then click on **Favorite Places**. A drop-down window opens and reveals the names and addresses of the favorite places.

You find favorite places by opening the Bookmarks section in the Windows Explorer. The bookmark folder is located in the Netscape directory folder (Figure 19) and can be found using the following steps:

1. Click on **Start**.
2. Move the pointer to **Programs**.
3. Locate the **Windows Explorer** and click on it.
4. Locate the Netscape folder. If you can't find the Netscape folder, click on **Program Files** or use the **Find** feature discussed earlier or consult your Windows manual.
5. Double-click on the **Netscape** file folder icon.
6. Double-click on the **Navigator** folder.

7. Locate **Bookmarks** and double-click on it. This should display the entire list of bookmarks. Moving the mouse pointer over the bookmarks should cause the URL to be displayed in the lower left corner of the computer screen. Write down these hypertext links and use them to visit those particular sites for more information.

! ● **CAUTION: Browsers often include a large number of startup bookmarks to preselected sites. These bookmarks are not created by the user and may be of little use to the investigator. Bookmarks set up by the individual computer user are more important.**

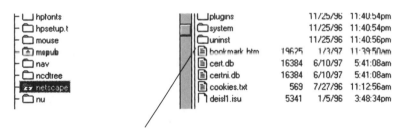

Fig. 19   Bookmark location in Netscape.

The investigator may also be able to retrieve waiting e-mail messages. Let's take the case of a runaway girl as an example. There may be messages with important clues as to the whereabouts or motives of the runaway. There are three types of e-mail messages: the new message, the old message, and the saved (or trashed) message. The first type is the new e-mail message, the one that has not been read by the addressee. To access this kind of message, the investigator must log on to the computer and retrieve the new message. It is a good idea to use a different computer to retrieve new messages. In other words, if possible get the log-on name and password and then get the e-mail message using another computer. Using the actual computer is easier and faster, but downloading new messages may overwrite existing information.

The second type of e-mail message is one that has already been read. You can often uncover prior e-mail messages by going to the mail menu of the Internet browser. While there may be slight variations among browsers and programs, I will guide you through an example using Netscape. You can find both sent and received e-mail messages in Netscape running under Windows 95 using the following steps:

1. Move the pointer to **Start** and click.
2. Move the mouse to **Programs**.
3. Find the **Netscape** folder and click on it.
4. From the Navigator window double-click on **Netscape**.
5. Click on **Window**, located on the task bar.
6. From the drop-down window, click on **Netscape Mail**. (If you get a message telling you that Netscape is unable to locate the server, click **OK** and this window should disappear.)
7. You should now be at the Netscape Mail window. Note the Mail Folder window on the left hand side. You should see three file folder icons: one for *Inbox*, one for **Sent**, and one for *Trash*. To see the sent e-mail messages click on **Sent**.
8. A new window appears on the right-hand side with icons of envelopes. Click on one of the envelopes.
9. A new window opens near the bottom of the Netscape Mail window. Use the scroll-down arrows on the right to read this message. Note that this window not only displays the e-mail message, but also the date, time, sender, addressee, and the address to which the e-mail was sent. That can be a lot of useful information.

Repeat the steps above to select the Inbox and you have access to recently received e-mail messages, or select the Trash folder to access either of these e-mail repositories.

E-mail messages can also be uncovered through the File Manager (Figure 20) or in the Windows 95 Explorer. The following steps are used in Netscape:

1. Move the pointer to **Start** and click.
2. Move the mouse to **Programs**.
3. Find the **Windows Explorer** and click on it.
4. Find the Netscape folder (it may be in the Program Files folder, in which case you will have to click on **Program Files**).
5. Once you have found Netscape, double-click on it.
6. Double-click on **Navigator**.
7. Look for the **Mail** folder and double-click on it.
8. Look for folders named Inbox, Sent, and Trash. You may find that a number of folders are named Inbox, Sent, and Trash. Look in the window under Type. The files you want to open are the ones designated as "File." The file type is listed to the right of the file name and file size.
9. Once you find a file of the "File" type, double-click on it.
10. You will probably get a message that this file needs to be associated ("Opened With") with a program such as the Write program in Windows 3.1 or Word Pad in Windows 95. We have already discussed how to associate files. Check with your operating system manual for details on how to associate files. You'll find that associating this file with Word Pad or Write will open and display the contents of the messages.

| inbox | 3546 | 1/8/96 | 8:07:34pm |
| sent | 0 | 1/5/96 | 4:37:26pm |

Fig. 20

Disk Detective

Going through File Manager or Winfile has one additional advantage. You may be able to thwart password protection features that are activated when the actual program is loaded. You may also be able to get around passwords by printing the contents of mail files directly from File Manager or from Winfile. This may involve renaming the file and then associating the file with a suitable program, such as Microsoft Word. Here's one example of how this was done on my computer.

1. Move the pointer to **Start** and click on it.
2. Move the mouse to **Programs**.
3. Find the **Windows Explorer** and click on it.
4. Find the **Program Files** folder and double-click on it.
5. Find the **Netscape** folder and double-click on it.
6. Find the **Navigator** folder and double-click on it.
7. Find the **Mail** folder and double-click on it.
8. Look for Files of the "File" type named either *Inbox, Sent,* or *Trash.*
9. Click on one of these files. For example, to find information in the Trash folder, click on **Trash**.
10. Click on **File**.
11. Click on **Open With** (see Figure 17).
12. Click on a program (e.g., Wordpad) and click **OK**.
13. This should open the Trash file. You can then read the message or select **Print** from the File menu to print the contents of the Trash file.

You can locate e-mail directories for various browsers by using Windows Find feature (**Start/Find/Files or Folders**). A good place to begin is by searching for *.mbx (mailbox) files. You can also search for files named inbox or outbox. A likely candidate for the location of mail files is the Express/Mail directory in the Microsoft Outlook folder. Juno mail may be in "User" folders in the Juno directory. Eudora stores mail in the Eudora directory, etc. A little detective work will help locate these mail directories.

Retracing Visited Internet Sites

Now, a few final words about downloaded files. People download all kinds of information from the Internet, including software programs, games, files, and photographs. Downloaded information is usually stored in a subdirectory or folder called download. I say usually because a user can select any folder on his computer to accept downloaded information. Figure 18 shows the location of a typical download subdirectory. You can find the download directory by using the Find feature in Windows 95 by clicking on Start, then clicking on **Find**, and then clicking on **Files or Folders**. In the Named: dialogue box, type in the word download and click on **Find Now**. This should bring up the Download directory and display the files that were downloaded. Use an appropriate program to open the downloaded files. Remember browsers are different and a little detective work may be needed to find these files and directories.

Another favorite practice of Internet surfers is to snatch pictures from visited sites. Suppose someone visits a particular site and likes one of the pictures on that site. It is extremely easy to copy such a picture by clicking right on the image then selecting **Save Image As . . .** The image will then be copied to the user's computer in a folder such as the Favorites folder. The following steps find pictures stored in the Favorites folder:

1. Click on **Start**.
2. Move the pointer to **Programs**.
3. Find the **Windows Explorer** and click on it.
4. Find the **Windows** folder and click on it.
5. Find the **Favorites** folder and double-click on it.
6. Look for file names with GIF or JPEG images.
7. Double-click on one of these files. This should open one of Window's programs and display the picture.

The computer user may have designated another folder to

receive these pictures. To find the location of the last designated folder set by the computer user, do the following:

1. Log on to the Internet using the actual computer.
2. Go to any site that has pictures or graphics.
3. Move the pointer to any picture or graphic.
4. Right click the mouse.
5. Move the pointer to **Save Image As . . .** and click.
6. A Save As . . . dialogue box appears. Look at the dialogue box next to **Save in**. This is the last folder that was used to store pictures. Write down the name of the folder. You can click on the file folder icon next to the Save in: dialogue box, and it will reveal more information about the folders in which the pictures are stored. Exit the browser.
7. Click on **Start**.
8. Move the pointer to **Find**.
9. Move the pointer to **Files or Folders** and click.
10. Type in the name of the folder you wrote down in step 6 and enter it at the cursor location.
11. Click on **Find Now**.
12. Windows searches for all folders matching the name you entered. You'll have to find the correct folder from the list. Double-click on this folder and it should display a list of pictures

Most programs have folders or directories named cookies. Cookies collect information about online activities and monitor visits to various Internet sites. Cookies provide companies with feedback about what kind of information the user is interested in. Cookies may also provide some insights about online activities.

You can glimpse inside the cookies folder using the following steps in Windows 95:

1. Click on **Start**.
2. Move the cursor to **Find**.
3. Move the cursor to **Files or Folders**.
4. Click on **Files or Folders**.
5. In the Find dialogue box type the word cookies and click on **Find Now**.
6. Windows searches and several cookies folders should appear, including a text file located in a folder such as **C:\Program Files\Netscape**.
7. Click on the **C:\Program Files\Netscape** folder. The cookie file should open. You may be able to obtain some useful information about online activities by checking out this file.

We wrap up this chapter with a brief discussion about a software tool called Triple Exposure that keeps track of where users have been on the Internet. Triple Exposure scans for pictures and movies and other material as defined by the individual who sets up the program. Such a program can be very useful for an investigator or parent who wants to keep track of Internet activities.

The objective of this chapter was to outline the kind of information that can be recovered from personal computers about online activities. Remember that browsers and individual user configurations may be different, and a little detective work may be required to locate this information on computers with other configurations. You also need to be aware that the privacy of certain electronic communications is protected by law. You can get into lots of trouble eavesdropping or retrieving certain information. Consult an attorney before doing anything.

The next chapter will explore some of the issues related to passwords and password recovery methods.

Chapter Six

Password Recovery

It is common today for computer users to keep their data from prying eyes by protecting information and computer access with passwords. Passwords are like electronic locks that keep most people from accessing your computer. Password protection features are included in almost all off-the-rack computers. Such popular software programs as Microsoft Word, Quicken, and QuickBooks also include password protection features. Protecting one's files with passwords is sensible, especially in an environment where more than one person has access to the computer. A manager in a large office would be smart to protect his (or her) privacy with passwords. Logic, however, tells us that passwords cannot be foolproof. People forget their passwords all the time. Yet somehow few people actually lose their data due to a forgotten password. Therefore, there must obviously be ways to circumvent passwords.

Passwords can be circumvented in a number of ways. Without special software, however, it can be virtually impossible to crack a carefully crafted password. Take the password EiKlcEitsT. This is a good password. How long would it take to go through all possible combinations of this 10 character password?

Assuming the average life span of a human being is 75 years and you were to enter a 10-letter password every second of a person's life, you wouldn't even come close to going through all the possible combinations. Despite these seemingly overwhelming odds, passwords are cracked every day.

EiKlcEitsT is an example of a good password. It is not an English word and therefore thwarts hackers who use special dictionaries to find passwords. Despite its seemingly nonsensical arrangement of characters, this password is quite easy to remember. This password is made up from the first letters of the phrase "Everyone i Know loves closing Escrows in the spring Time." The upper- and lower-case words follow a certain sequence. The first letter in the first word is capitalized followed by a lower-case word. The first letter of the third word is capitalized followed by two lower-case words. The first letter of the sixth word is capitalized followed by three lower-case words. It's as easy as 1, 2, 3. Of course, you can always throw in a number for good measure. All passwords should have at least one number to make things just a bit more difficult.

The problem is that most people don't select good passwords like EiKlcEitsT. Many computer users are careless in setting up their passwords. It's common for people to use passwords based on a common English word or to use the name of their spouse, one of their kids, their pet, or their address or Social Security number. This, of course, makes passwords easier to crack, even without special software.

People may also reverse common words, like changing their first name from Walter to retlaW. Then there are those who base passwords on favorite characters or actors. If someone has Elvis posters plastered all over the bedroom walls, chances are that his or her password will be something like Elvis, Elvis1, the king, or sivlE (that's Elvis spelled backwards).

An investigator should look around the computer area or desk space for clues about passwords. Many people write passwords down on paper and stick them in a drawer or post them on a cork board. A few minutes spent looking around the computer work area may be well spent. People may also confide passwords to close friends, family members, and co-workers.

Investigators will encounter all types of passwords. Just as there are a variety of locks that safeguard our homes and businesses, so too are there a variety of passwords that lock computers and computer files.

We begin our journey into password recovery by examining the first line of defense often employed to safeguard computer information: the CMOS password, sometimes called the BIOS password. If a CMOS password is set, a dialogue box pops up even before the computer boots up. Without knowing the CMOS password, the user is locked out. Some of you might be wondering if you can bypass the CMOS password by booting the computer from a bootable floppy, like Norton's Emergency Disk or a bootable DOS disk. This is a good thought, but it won't work. Without the CMOS password the computer never even gets to the floppy disk drive and therefore can't boot from it.

Despite its formidable-sounding name, the CMOS password is not infallible and can be thwarted—although this can be a bit tricky. The key to breaking the CMOS's password lies in the fact that CMOS memory is maintained by an electrical current usually supplied by a battery. Because CMOS needs a constant flow of electricity, the information in its memory, including the password, is volatile. This means that if the electricity to CMOS is interrupted long enough, the data stored in CMOS, including the password, will be gone.

This is good news and bad. The good news, obviously, is that the password will be gone. The bad news is that the password is not the only thing that will be erased. CMOS stores more than just the password. It stores such vital information as hard-disk type and configuration, as well as information about other devices. Once the CMOS power is erased, all of the CMOS information needs to be input again. If the CMOS information is inaccurate, the computer may not boot up or run properly. Then you will have eliminated the password along with the ability to log on the computer. Most computer professionals can get the computer up and running again.

❗ Another way to circumvent the CMOS password is to remove the entire disk and reinstall it in another compatible computer. Remember, though, that the other computer must be properly configured for the transplanted disk.

The CMOS configuration varies by type of computer and type of motherboard. Sometimes a switch or jumper is used to communicate with CMOS. Flipping the proper switch or removing the appropriate jumper will interrupt and reset CMOS to its original configuration, which is usually without a password. The investigator should check the computer or motherboard documentation for the location of the CMOS switch/jumper as well as the CMOS setup configurations.

You may be able to reset the CMOS to factory defaults by moving system board jumpers to clear CMOS and then restoring the jumpers to their original settings. Refer to the specific motherboard documentation for complete information.

Remember, the original CMOS information needs to be reentered after the CMOS power is interrupted. You must know the CMOS information, including hard-disk type, sectors, tracks, etc., before you disrupt the power.

Removing the CMOS battery causes CMOS's memory to lapse. It may take up to an hour, but the CMOS information, including the password, will be lost. After the CMOS information is erased, the computer will not boot up. Instead of booting, one or more error messages will fill the screen such as:

Password Recovery

- Battery Discharged
- Hard Disk # Error
- Hardware Information Does Not Match—Run SETUP
- Time and Date Corrupt—Run SETUP
- A variety of messages that end in "Run SETUP"

If you know how to program CMOS information back in, the computer will boot without the password. If you don't know how to program the correct CMOS settings, you're out of luck, and the computer will be inoperable. Taking the computer to a professional for CMOS work can save you lots of headaches.

The second password that will likely be encountered is the Windows 95 user-name password.

An easy password to circumvent is the Windows 95 user-name password. The user-name password dialogue box pops up just before the main Windows screen loads. To get into Windows, you have to type in the appropriate password. Typing in the wrong password and pressing Enter will keep you locked out of Windows forever. Simply clicking on Cancel, however, causes Windows to open right up. This trick, by the way, won't work on NT.

To understand the Windows user-name password, let's look at how to set one up in Windows 95.

1. Click on **Start**.
2. Move the cursor to **Settings** and click on **Control Panel**.
3. From the window that appears, look for the Passwords icon (a gold and two silver keys) and double-click on the **Password** icon.
4. A Passwords Properties window appears. From this window click on the **Change Windows Password . . .** button.
5. Enter a password in the New password dialogue box and confirm the password in the second dialogue box.
6. Click on **OK** and your password is set. The next time you start Windows, it will ask for your password.

It's that simple to set up a password. Next time Windows starts, a dialog box appears, along with the user's name and a password prompt. After a user establishes a password, Windows sets up a pwl file under the user's name. For example, let's assume that someone sets up a password under the user name Bobby. To activate the password, Windows sets up a file named Bobby.pwl. This file is located in the Windows Folder. To locate Windows pwl files, open the Explorer, go to the Windows folder, and look for a file named Bobby.pwl. If

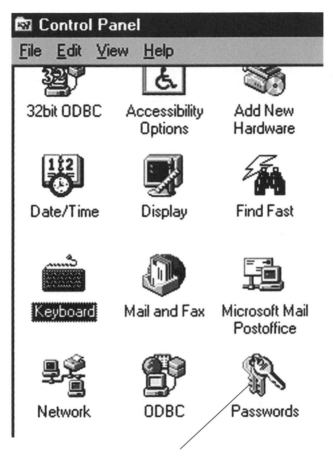

Fig. 21. The Password icon in control panel.

the Bobby.pwl file were to be deleted, the password would be gone. The next time Windows is rebooted, the computer user would be given a choice of either changing the user name, changing the password, or removing the password entirely. Though this is quite a simple step, there are some preference settings that may impact this procedure. Always refer to your Windows documentation for complete instructions.

Disk Detective

The next likely password one is likely to encounter is the Windows 95 screensaver password. As you probably know, screensavers are special programs (e.g., fish, flying toasters, flying windows) that are activated after a certain period of computer inactivity. Many people like screensavers. They provide some entertainment and protect the computer screen from burning out.

The Windows 95 screensaver is like many other screensavers. When someone stops working on a computer for a predetermined amount of time, the selected screensaver appears. In Windows 3.1 moving the mouse or pressing any key causes the screensaver to disappear, and the user is back to work. This is not the case in Windows 95. The Windows 95 screensaver can be password-protected. If the screensaver is activated, moving the mouse or pressing any key won't bring back the program(s). One must first enter the correct screen saver password before Windows lets you get back into the system.

There are two options to the screensaver dilemma. First, turn the computer off and reboot, and then keep on working on the computer so that the screensaver doesn't get the chance to kick in. Fortunately, there are other alternatives.

You can turn off the screensaver password from within Windows 95. Surprisingly, you don't have to know the user's screensaver password to change or deactivate the screensaver, at least not in the version used at the time of this writing. To delete the screensaver password:

1. Click on **Start** (you may have to reboot the computer first).
2. From the next window, click on **Settings**.
3. From the next window click on **Control Panel**.
4. From the Control Panel window, double-click on the Display icon (this is a small picture of a monitor with the word display beneath it).
5. From the Display Properties window, click on the **Screen Saver** tab.

6. If a screensaver password is set, the Display Properties window will have a check mark in the <u>P</u>assword-protected check box (Figure 22). Move the mouse pointer to the **Password-protected** check box and click on it. The check mark disappears.

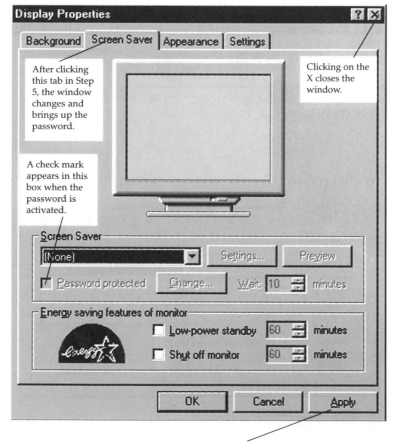

Fig. 22

After deselecting (or changing) the password options, click on **OK** or **Apply** to implement the changes.

7. Click on **Apply** in the lower right-hand side of the screen.
8. Close the window by clicking on the X located on the upper right-hand side of the window and the screensaver password is gone!

You can also use a screensaver password-cracking program like SsRecover. This program costs about $30 and will quickly reveal the screensaver passwords. You might wonder why anyone would pay $30 for a program that cracks the screensaver password, especially since it is so easy to disable the password feature. The reason is simple. Many people use the same password to protect a number of programs and files. Thus, once you uncover one password, you may have discovered the password to other programs. At the very least, you will have some idea as to the kind of password used. For example, suppose you find out that the screensaver password is Fred, which happens to be one of the names of the computer user's children. If the user has another child named Sue, it's a safe bet that Sue may be a password that protects other documents as well.

Using the same password for all computer documents is like having one key that fits all locks in an entire building. Once the investigator has this master key, he or she has access to the entire building. That's why setting just one password is a bad security procedure. However, computer users who are afraid of forgetting their passwords often settle for a single password or a slight variation of one password. That's why spending $30 on a program like Ss-Recover may be a good investment. You may find more than just the screensaver password, and you might just find the master key to get into all password-protected files.

Recovering the screensaver password with Ss-Recover is simple. The example below uses the Ss-Recover version 1.0 for Windows 95. Ss-Recover finds passwords for Windows 95 as well as *After Dark* screensavers. Recovered passwords are displayed in plain text. Ss-Recover has one other helpful feature. Even if the password mode is not currently selected, Ss-Recover searches for the last password used. This is also important to the investigator, because it can uncover valuable clues about password trends.

Ss-Recover is simple to use. The step-by-step process to uncover the screensaver password follows:

1. From Windows 95, put the Ss-Recover disk in drive A.
2. Click on **Start**.
3. Move the pointer to Programs. This opens the window of available programs.
4. From the program list, move the pointer to the **Windows Explorer** and click on it.
5. From the window find the icon for **My Computer** (C:) and click on it.
6. The right side of the next window displays a small "key" icon and the SsRecover program. Double-click on the **key** icon.
7. A small window appears. Double-click on **Get Password**.
8. Voila! The next screen displays the screensaver password.

Another password that is relatively easy to recover is the password for the DOS Shell. Many of today's computers do not have the DOS Shell, but recovering the DOS Shell passwords still deserves some attention.

DOS Shell is similar to the Windows File Manager and Explorer. Unlike File Manager and Explorer, however, the DOS Shell is a text-oriented interface with point-and-click features. In the later days of DOS, the shell made it easier for novice users to get things done.

DOS Shell has scroll boxes with bars, menus, and pull-down menus that represented an advance in DOS. Later versions of DOS dispensed with this shell altogether, though it was still available as a subsidiary program.

Since DOS Shell first previewed, a whole generation of computer users were weaned on Windows and probably don't even know about this prehistoric DOS feature. Remember, at one time computer users did not have colorful user interfaces like Windows. Early computer users were faced with the intimidating C:\> prompt. To get a computer to do anything at all, you had to know exacting DOS syntax.

DOS Shell allows users to set up passwords. But DOS Shell passwords are not encrypted and are easy to recover. Recovering a DOS Shell password has several benefits to the investigator.

We have already discussed that users often select similar passwords. Thus if the investigator can find one password, like the one used in the DOS Shell, he or she may have found the master key that will unlock other files or provide important clues as to the password trends.

There are several ways to uncover DOS Shell passwords. Those with a spirit for adventure and lots of time can search through the disk with a text-string search option like the one found in Norton Utilities (text string searches will be outlined in later chapters).

A text string search stops at all references to a selected word. Thus, doing a text string search on the word *password* causes the computer to stop at all references to *password*. You may be able to find passwords using this method. Searching for references to *password* on a hard disk can take many hours. There are thousands of references to the text string *password*. Every program, such as DOS, Windows, QuickBooks, or Word, has numerous references that contain the text string *password*, and Norton Utilities' Disk Editor stops at all of them. An easier and faster method for recovering the DOS Shell password is examined below:

After finding the password, continue scrolling through the pages until you get back to the DOS prompt.

Password Recovery

To recover a password in DOS Shell, first change to the DOS prompt. Your screen should look like this:

C:\>

Change to the DOS directory by typing **cd dos** and pressing **Enter**. The next screen should now look like this:

C:\DOS>

At the C:\DOS> prompt, type: **type dosshell.ini | more** and then press **Enter**. The character immediately after ".ini" is the pipe character. The pipe character consists of two small vertical dashes, one on top of the other. On most keyboards, the pipe character is located on the key that contains the back slash (\) character.

When the **dosshell.ini | more** command is entered, a screen of information flows across the monitor. Press the **Enter** key and the next part of the dosshell.ini file will fill the screen. Keep pressing the **Enter** key until a reference to the password appears. The password reference will look something like this:

```
}
program =                              The password (podpeop)
{                                      is revealed several pages down
help = password is podpeop             into the dosshell.ini file.
screenmode = text
alttab = enabled
ctrlesc = enabled
```

Fig. 23

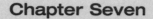

Chapter Seven

More About Passwords

Passwords represent one of the most significant obstacles in computer investigation. This chapter will focus on recovering passwords with common password recovery programs, such as those offered by Access Data and Crack software. Password recovery software can also be obtained over the Internet, though these programs are usually for older versions of software.

I actually like some of the older programs; they don't have a lot of bells, whistles, and pretty graphics, but they are pretty effective. I have acquired several impressive shareware recovery programs for free simply by searching the Internet and downloading the files. You can find an astonishing array of file crackers, including ones for Trumpet Winsock, Excel, WordPerfect, Zip, UNIX, Windows, and many others. Most of the files are in zip format, and the user must first use an unzip program on these files before they can be used. Downloading files over the Internet is also accompanied by the risk that they could contain a virus. Be sure you have a virus-checking program with current definitions before downloading anything.

For serious investigations, however, there is nothing better than password-recovery programs sold by reputable firms.

Disk Detective

These programs are designed for today's newest software and offer product and user support. Some of these password recovery programs are designed specifically for law enforcement professionals. Most of these programs are sold for the sole purpose of helping individuals who have forgotten their password or companies that have legitimate reasons to access their password-protected documents, such as when an employee leaves the firm, leaving behind protected documents. **NOTE:** Reference to any password-recovery program in this book does not imply that the vendor intends that its software be used for investigative purposes. You should contact the vendor for suitable uses of its programs.

To help understand how to recover passwords, we'll first take a look at how to set up a password in Microsoft Word. We use Word as an example, although other password recovery programs work in similar ways. Since it is beyond the scope of this book to outline all password-recovery programs on the market, we have to limit our examples to just this one program.

This book was written using Word, a sophisticated word processing program from Microsoft. Like many of today's popular software programs, Word has security features, including the ability to set up passwords. The ability to protect confidential work is a nice feature in any program. Word's password-protection feature is quite sophisticated and relatively easy to use. Under normal circumstances the password-protection feature built into Word does a fine job of protecting documents. That does not mean, however, that Word's password protection is infallible.

Protecting a Word document with a password is relatively simple. The following are the directions for Word 6.0 running under Windows 3.1:

1. Open the document that you wish to password protect.
2. Click on the **File** menu.

3. Click on **Save As** . . . (if the file has not been previously saved, enter a file name and then proceed to step 4).
4. Click the **Options** button.
5. Enter the password in the Protection Password dialogue box and press **OK**.
6. Type in the password again.
7. After reentering the password (see Figure 24), click **OK**.

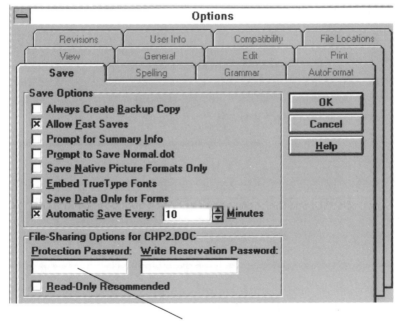

Fig. 24   Enter a password here and click OK.

The process for setting a password for Microsoft Word for Windows 95 is virtually identical, except that the windows and dialogue boxes in Windows 95 are a little different. To protect a document in Word for Windows 95, do the following:

1. Open the document you wish to protect.

2. Click on the **File** menu.
3. Click on **Save As . . .** (if the file has not been previously saved, enter a file name and proceed to step 4).
4. Click the **Options** button.
5. Enter a password in the **Password to open** dialogue box and click **OK**.
6. Reenter the password.
7. After reentering the password in the dialogue box when prompted, click **OK**.

It's that simple to protect a Word document with a password. The password can contain up to 15 characters, consisting of letters (both upper and lower case), numbers, symbols, and spaces. Once a password is assigned, the user must type in the password for the document to open.

! **Some readers are probably wondering if one can still access information in a password-protected file by using the Norton Disk Editor. The answer is no. The Editor cannot read these password-protected files because Word actually encrypts these files based on the chosen password.**

Despite seeming like a formidable barrier, passwords in many popular programs can be recovered. It is, however, extremely difficult, if not impossible, for an everyday computer user to crack a well-conceived password without special software or special skills. With the right password-recovery program, however, passwords can be recovered in a matter of seconds.

There are a number of programs that are designed to recover passwords. From the user's perspective, most password-recovery programs work very similarly. The process starts by inserting the password-recovery disk and following the directions that accompany the program. We will demonstrate how to recover the Word password with a program called WDPASS from AccessData. The following are the directions for recovering the password from Word version 6 running under Windows 3.1:

1. Place the AccessData WDPASS disk in drive A.
2. Type **a:wdpass** at the DOS prompt and press **Enter**.
3. After the program description and utility screen appear, read the information and press **Enter** to continue.
4. Enter the access code that accompanies the WDPASS program and press **Enter**.
5. You will be prompted for the name and path of the locked file. For example, the file name for this chapter is chp2.doc. This file is located in a subdirectory named Paladin in the Winword directory on drive C. Thus the complete path statement is **C:\Winword\Paladin\chp2.doc**.
6. After typing in the correct path name, press **Enter**.
7. Another utility screen appears, prompting you for the version of Word that created the file. (If you do not know which version was used, open Word and click on **Help**. From the dialogue box, click on **About Microsoft Word . . .**, which will display the current Word version.) For example, to open this chapter, which was written with Word 6.0, you would select MSWORD 6.x from WDPASS's list of options. After highlighting the proper version, press **Enter**.
8. The next screen contains a status bar that keeps you informed of the password-recovery progress. It takes just a few minutes for WDPASS to identify the correct password.
9. After the password is recovered, close down WDPASS and open the Word program.
10. In the password dialogue box (Figure 25), type in the name of the recovered password. The document will now open.

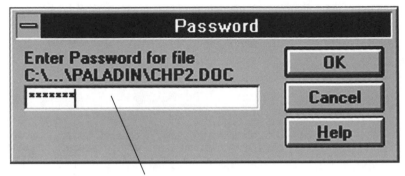

Fig. 25   Password dialog box in word. A password is required to
open the file or to change the password.

WDPASS has other features that allow you to find File
Sharing passwords from Microsoft Word. The program referenced here is actually an older version. I have had the opportunity to preview its new password-recovery software and
have found its features vastly enhanced.

There are a number of commercially available password-
recovery programs, including those for MS Word, WordPerfect,
Quicken, MS Excel, MS Money, Lotus, Paradox, Windows
Screensaver, AMI BIOS, Trumpet Winsock, and many more.
Keep in mind that most of these programs were designed to be
used by people who have lost or forgotten their passwords.

AccessData makes a special law enforcement password-
recovery package, but it is not available to the general public.

One thing to keep in mind about password recovery and
other investigative programs is to avoid installing the password-recovery software on the hard disk of the computer
being investigated. Loading any software, including data-
recovery or password-recovery programs, on a computer may
overwrite information that may have been recoverable.

If you must install password-recovery software on a hard
disk, do so on another computer that contains an exact duplicate of the disk being investigated.

You can also recover passwords by using what is called a

backdoor approach. The following is an example for Quicken 3.0. In an earlier chapter, we discussed how Windows stores passwords in pwl files. Quicken 3.0 stores files in QDT. By using an editor, such as Norton Utilities, these files can be edited by zeroing out the appropriate offsets on the disk, which is a process best left to experienced data-recovery professionals.

Chapter Eight

Other Tips and Tricks

There are a number of tips and tricks that can help the investigator uncover other computer activities. It may be helpful, for example, for an investigator to know which computer files were accessed most recently. Many programs, such as Microsoft Word, actually display the most recently used files. When you open Word, for example, a list of the most recently opened documents is displayed after selecting the File option from the menu bar.

Word is by no means the only program that lists the most recent files. Most of today's popular software lists the recently used files. A photo-editing program, for example, will list files that contain the most recently accessed photographs or images. The most recently used files can be an important source of determining the state of mind of an individual. For example, suppose an adult vanishes without a trace. Looking at his or her most recently used files may reveal important clues as to his or her whereabouts. Someone in financial trouble may have accessed accounting records numerous times. A wife who may have run away with a new lover may have used a word processing program to write love letters. A serial killer may have opened graphic violent images in his photo program prior to committing his last murder.

One can also use File Manager and Windows Explorer to find the most recently accessed files. In Windows 95, for example, you can quickly find the 15 most recently opened documents by clicking **Start** and then clicking on the **Documents** folder. This displays a window that lists the most recently opened files. You can open these documents to see the file's contents by clicking on any of the documents in the Documents folder.

Another neat trick in Windows helps the investigator determine when a document was created and when it was last modified. If a minor disappears, for example, it would be important to know what files were accessed prior to the child's disappearance. Knowing what files were opened can provide valuable insight as to the state of mind of the runaway or yield other important clues as to his or her whereabouts. It is also important to know when these documents were created, as well as when they were modified and accessed. All of this is easy in Windows 95. Once you have determined the names and locations of the most recently opened files in the Documents folder, do the following:

1. Open the Windows Explorer. Find the file(s) that have been recently opened. Move your mouse over a file name and click the right mouse button.
2. From the drop-down window that appears, click on **Properties**.
3. A window will open and display a variety of information, such as when the file was created, when it was modified, and when it was last accessed. Clicking on the Summary tab displays the author's name (as determined by the computer). The Statistics tab displays the number of times the document has been revised and other statistical information about the document.

Files in the Explorer can be arranged in a variety of ways that can help the investigator. You can list files by name, file type, file size, and file date. Displaying files by the date they were last modified can lead the investigator to the most recently accessed documents. The following steps will order files by date in the Windows 95 Explorer:

1. Move the pointer to **Start**.
2. Move the pointer to **Programs**.
3. Move the pointer to **Windows Explorer** and click.
4. In the right-hand window, look for the folder(s) that contains the files you are interested in and double-click on that folder.
5. Click on **View**.
6. Move the pointer to **Arrange Icons**.
7. Move the pointer to by **Date** and click.

The files will then be listed with the most recently accessed files (or folders) on top.

File Manager in Windows 3.1 has several handy features that point the investigator in the right direction. File Manager's View menu lets you change the way files are listed. You can display files in ascending or descending order by date, file name, file size, or file type. For example, to find out which word processing document was opened most recently do the following:

1. Double-click on **File Manager** (usually found in the main menu of Program Manager).
2. Locate the directory that contains the files you are interested in.
3. Double-click on the subdirectory that contains the files you are interested in.

4. Click on **V**iew.
5. Click on **Sort by** **D**ate.

The Windows File Manager displays the most recently accessed file at the top of the list.

Computers operating under DOS can be made to display a variety of information with the **DIR** command. Typing DIR at the DOS prompt lists the volume label and serial number of the disk. The DIR command also displays the file name, extension, number of bytes, last date the file was edited, and time when the file was edited.

To list the most recently accessed files in DOS, you have to use an attribute switch. This sounds difficult, but it is pretty simple. For example, using the /O switch with the DIR command lets you select the order in which the files are listed. To get DOS to display files by date, type **DIR/OD**. This is how this line would look on your computer screen.

C:\>DIR/OD

There are a number of other options for displaying files in DOS. You can get full details by typing **help dir** at the DOS prompt:

C:\>help dir

HIDDEN ATTRIBUTES

Because we are discussing switches, this may be a good time to discuss the hidden attribute switch. Some individuals can "bury" files on disk by assigning a hidden attribute. After the hidden attribute is assigned, the file is no longer listed in DOS, Windows File Manager, or in the Explorer. Here is what may happen if the investigator forgets the possible existence of hidden files. The investigator picks up a floppy disk and puts it in drive A. He or she clicks on the A icon in File Manager (or the Explorer) and gets a "no files found" message. It would be a mistake to assume that there is no information on the disk. In fact, the disk could be chockful of all kinds of information, including files, deleted files, and information remaining in slack space. Let's look at how to assign a hidden attribute to a file or folder and then we'll learn how to find and display files that have the hidden attribute set.

HIDING A FILE WITH THE HIDDEN ATTRIBUTE—WINDOWS 95

1. Click on **Start**.
2. Move the pointer to **Programs**.
3. Move the pointer to **Windows Explorer** and click once.
4. Click on the file to which you wish to assign a hidden attribute.
5. Click on **File**.
6. Click on **Properties**.
7. Click on **Hidden** from the Properties window and click **OK**.

Usually, the file for which the hidden attribute has been set will disappear from the screen. Whether a hidden file disappears or remains on the screen depends on the preferences that have been set in the **View** and **Options** menus. For example, if you set the hidden attribute for a file in Windows 95 and it still remains on the screen, then the options in the View menu have been set to display all files, including those that have the hidden attribute set. Obviously, however, someone going through the process of hiding files is going to be clever enough to set the Windows 95 option so that hidden files will not displayed.

DISPLAYING FILES WITH HIDDEN ATTRIBUTES IN WINDOWS 95

1. Click on **Start**.
2. Move the pointer to **Programs**.

3. Move the mouse to **Windows Explorer** and click once.
4. Click on **View** in the menu bar.
5. From the drop-down window click on **Options**.
6. Click on **Show all files**.
7. Click on **OK**.

This causes the files, including those with the hidden attributes, to be displayed.

HIDING A FILE WITH
THE HIDDEN ATTRIBUTE—WINDOWS 3.1

1. Double-click on **File Manager**.
2. Click on the file to which you wish to assign the hidden attribute.
3. Click on **File** from the menu bar.
4. Click on **Properties**.
5. Click on the **Hidden Attribute** box.
6. Click on **OK**.

The file that has the hidden attribute assigned should disappear from the list of displayed files.

DISPLAYING FILES WITH
HIDDEN ATTRIBUTES IN WINDOWS 3.1

1. Open the Windows **File Manager**.
2. Click on **View** from the menu bar.
3. Click on **By File Type**.
4. Click on **Show Hidden/System Files**.
5. Click on **OK**.

This causes the files, including those with the hidden attribute, to be displayed.

HIDING A FILE BY ASSIGNING
THE HIDDEN ATTRIBUTE—DOS 6.2

The following steps set the hidden attribute for files in DOS. For this example, we will assume that the target file named "hideit" is located in the Paladin subdirectory of the Winword directory.

1. At the DOS prompt, change to the directory that contains the file for which you want to set the hidden attribute. In our example, this is the Winword directory. We change to the Winword **directory by typing cd winword at the DOS prompt and pressing** Enter. After changing to the new directory, the DOS prompt looks like this: **C:\WINWORD>**
2. Next, change to the subdirectory named Paladin. To do so type **cd paladin** at the **C:\WINWORD>** prompt and press **Enter**. The DOS prompt now looks like this: **C:\WINWORD\PALADIN>**
3. At the C:\WINWORD\PALADIN> prompt type **dir/w/p** and press **Enter**.
4. This causes the list of files in the C:\WINWORD\PALADIN> directory, including the "hideit" file, to be displayed. Now, to set the hidden attribute of the "hideit" file type **attrib +h hideit**.
5. Press **Enter**.
6. Type **dir/w/p** again and you will note that the "hideit" file is no longer displayed.

DISPLAYING FILES INCLUDING
THOSE WITH HIDDEN ATTRIBUTES IN DOS

1. At the DOS prompt, change to the directory that contains the file(s) that may have the hidden attribute set. In our example, this is the Winword directory. Change to the

Winword directory by typing **cd winword** at the DOS prompt. After changing to the new directory, the DOS prompt looks like this: **C:\WINWORD>**

2. Next, change to the subdirectory named Paladin by typing **cd paladin** at the **C:\WINWORD>** prompt. The DOS prompt now looks like this: **C:\WINWORD\PALADIN>**

3. At the C:\WINWORD\PALADIN> prompt type **attrib**

4. This causes a list of files, including those with hidden attributes, to be displayed. The list of files will look something like this:

H   C:\WINWORD\PALADIN\HIDEIT.DOC
H   C:\WINWORD\PALADIN\CHP1.DOC
A H C:\WINWORD\PALADIN\CHP2.DOC

All the files that have the letter H are hidden files that would normally not be displayed. Now, let's take a look at how to clear the hidden attribute from a file.

5. At the DOS prompt, change to the directory that contains the file for which you want to set the hidden attribute. In our example, this is the Winword directory. We change to the Winword directory by typing **cd winword** at the DOS prompt. After changing to the new directory, the DOS prompt looks like this: **C:\WINWORD>**

6. Next, change to the subdirectory named Paladin. To do so, type **cd paladin** at the **C:\WINWORD>** prompt. The new DOS prompt now looks like this: **C:>WINWORD\PALADIN>**

7. At the C:>WINWORD\PALADIN> prompt type **attrib | more**. The character between attrib and more is the pipe character located on the same key as the \ character. The |more key will pause the flow of information after one screen, otherwise data cannot be read. Press Enter after each screen to see the next page of information.

8. This causes the list of files in the C:\WINWORD\PAL-ADIN> directory, including the "hideit file," to be displayed. Now, to clear the hidden attribute from the hideit file, type **attrib -h hideit**.
9. Press **Enter**.
10. Type **dir/w/p** again and you will note that the "hideit" file is now displayed.

We have examined several ways to display recently opened files and to uncover files that have been hidden by changing the file attribute. More information about attributes can be found by typing **help attrib** at the DOS prompt.

Another handy investigative utility is a keystroke recorder. Once loaded, this little device will record everything typed on the keyboard. Thus, when such a program is loaded on a computer, all keystrokes including passwords are recorded and kept in a special file. One such program is KEYLOG-WN for Windows 3.1 and Windows 95. This program can be run from the Startup Group and will not show up on the task bar. The commercial version of this program stores the keystrokes in a hidden directory that can be accessed later. Keystroke recording programs come in many varieties, but all have one purpose: to record all keystrokes. In that sense, these recorders are similar to typewriter ribbons that record all strokes made on the typewriter. Even words that are backspaced don't avoid detection. We do not imply that such programs are specifically for investigative purposes; they can be used to provide valuable backup for a word processing document. Yet their application to investigation, when done within the law, becomes irresistible.

Next, a word about programs that hide text files within graphic or audio files is in order. Most computer users wishing to protect information from others do so by means of assigning passwords or encrypting files. You should be aware, though, that there are software programs that hide text information inside audio and graphics files. These programs are relatively easy to use, and many can be obtained over the Internet. Suppose that you examine the contents of a floppy disk, and File Manager or Explorer reveals a .GIF file. Upon opening it, you find a picture of the Statue of Liberty. You should be aware that this file can have a message implanted within it. This message will not show up when the picture is opened.

Finally, investigators should be aware of such programs as Instant Print Screen that allow them to send whatever is on the screen to the printer. This feature can come in really handy when there is an image or information on the screen that you want to keep a record of. Such programs cost between $15 and $50 and may be well worth the expense. The other alternative is to take pictures of the screen with a camera, which is much more expensive and time consuming.

Conclusion

I hope you have found this publication helpful in understanding the fundamental framework for what kind of information can be recovered from computers as well as the basic framework that makes information recovery possible. Many factors were taken into account when writing this book, including the vast differences in individual computer skills and experience. The information here may be too technical for some readers and too basic for very experienced computer users. Unfortunately, there is no way to write a book such as this and appeal to all readers. Most parents, teachers, private investigators, and law enforcement professionals should have a better understanding about the kind of information that resides on computer storage media and the fundamental processes by which such information is retrieved. Police officers should have a much better awareness of the kind of evidence that resides on computers.

Forensic computer investigation is a complex task and must only be performed by a trained data recovery professional after consultation with an attorney who is knowledgeable in these matters. Please seek the advice of a data recovery expert and legal counsel before proceeding with any computer investigation. Remember, the examples in this book are *for illustrative purposes only*; they may not work on other computers with different configurations, operating systems, user preference settings, or newer versions of software.

I encourage you to visit my Web site at the following address: **http://www.diskdetectives.com**. I'll try to post any relevant reader comments and suggestions and updates on this site. I also wish to thank Paladin Press for making this book possible.